Diana Peacock has been making sweets and treats for her family or to give away as presents for nearly 30 years. She is also the author of *Everyday Family Favourites*, *Good Home Baking*, *Traditional Country Preserving* and co-author of *Grandma's Ways for Modern Days*.

Rebecca Peacock is a professional designer and keen cook. She is the author of *Make & Mend: A Guide to Recycling Clothes and Fabrics*.

Also available

HOW TO MAKE
SWEETS
AND
TREATS

Diana and Rebecca Peacock

ROBINSON

ROBINSON

Originally published in 2012 as *Sweets and Treats to Give Away* by Spring Hill

This edition published in Great Britain in 2014 by Robinson

A CIP catalogue record for this book is available from the British Library.

ISBN 978-0-71602-373-9 (paperback)
ISBN 978-0-71602-379-1 (ebook)

Typeset in Great Britain by Ian Hughes – www.mousematdesign.com
Printed and bound in Great Britain by CPI Group (UK) Ltd, Croydon, CR0 4YY

Robinson
is an imprint of
Constable & Robinson Ltd
100 Victoria Embankment
London EC4Y 0DY

An Hachette UK Company
www.hachette.co.uk

www.constablerobinson.com

Contents

Introduction to Making Sweets and Treats

A little effort and planning can ensure that the next gift you give will be not only delicious, but so impressive it will be spoken of for months. A good batch of homemade fudge will provide hours of delight as your recipient steals a cube or two to have with a cup of tea, all the while thinking how clever you are for making it, how thoughtful a gift it was and when will you make them some more. The great thing about making sweets as gifts is you can tailor the treat to the recipient, unlike buying them off the shelf, including their favourite flavours and leaving out any ingredients they might not enjoy. The magic of cooking with sugar makes the process all the more fun, and you can make the presents as expensive or economical as you wish.

This book aims to show you how a little planning and a few carefully selected but easily available ingredients can help you create a whole hamper of sweet treats that even the most difficult-to-buy-for friends and family will love.

Before You Start

Please be careful when cooking with sugar: the temperatures involved are not only very high, but a splash of boiling sugar can cause a serious injury as it continues to boil on the skin. Always use good quality utensils to ensure not only the best results but also to assist you in cooking as safely as possible. Always use a long-handled spoon or spatula as this keeps your hands well away from the boiling sugar.

Keep all pans and bowls of hot sugar as far away from children as possible. Although it might seem like a wonderful thing to do with the kids, cooking with sugar is extremely dangerous. There are a few projects in this book that are perfectly safe and fun to do with children, but ensure all boiled sugar projects are strictly adults only. It's much better to be safe than sorry!

Useful Hints

A lot of these tips become obvious with experience, but they are listed here so you don't have to wait! Here are some useful hints to get the best results first time.

- Baking paper or silicone-coated paper makes life a lot easier when cooling your sweet treats, as they don't stick to the paper and it means you don't have to grease any baking trays. Paper is also useful for baking. Lightly grease the tins before lining with paper as this stops it from slipping.

- Have everything weighed and ready to use before starting your recipe. This is especially useful when the timings of cooking sugar are important.

- If you are coating nuts in toffee, warm them in the oven gently first as the toffee will adhere to the nuts better.

- After cooking sugar place the used pan and utensils in very hot soapy water. The sugar will dissolve and cleaning them becomes effortless.

- When packing sweets in jars or tins, place a piece of crumpled silicone paper at the base and as a cover before replacing the lid. This will stop them breaking up or chipping.

- Wrap sweets and chocolates as soon as they are cool to ensure the longest possible shelf life.

- When working with chocolate keep your hands as cool as possible.

- Never allow water to splash into melting chocolate as this will cause it to thicken and go grainy.

- For an accurate reading on a thermometer, stand it upright in the sugar syrup and ensure the bulb is completely covered. Sugar thermometers usually have a base that raises them off the pan base, but if yours doesn't, try not to rest it on the bottom.

- Be patient. Gradually cooking sugar allows you to be more accurate in reading temperatures. Depending on the atmospheric conditions, sometimes the chemical processes will take longer than you think.

- Store your homemade sweets in an airtight container as soon as they are suitably cool. Individually wrapping will give you longer-lasting sweets.

Useful Utensils

You will not need a great deal of equipment for making sweets and treats. There are one or two utensils that are completely necessary though, and it is a good idea to get the best possible quality you can afford for achieving the best results as safely as possible.

The essentials
- A sturdy pan – not an enamel pan as they don't withstand heat. Use a stainless steel one with a copper base or double thickness steel base. This will ensure even cooking of sugar without burning.
- A long-handled spatula and wooden spoon.
- A sugar thermometer – this is very useful and takes the guessing out of the job.
- Silicone paper or baking paper – so you don't need to worry about constant greasing.
- Square and rectangular shallow baking tins – these are useful for fudge and caramel. They don't need to be non-stick if you line them with silicone paper or foil. Greasing the tin a little first will ensure the paper doesn't move about when you are filling the tin.

- Paper muffin, bun and petit four cases.
- Accurate scales.
- A fine sieve for dusting icing sugar.
- A good pair of scissors for cutting toffee and boiled sweets.
- A large knife for chopping up fudge and caramels.

Other equipment
You may also find the following equipment useful, though you'll manage without it.

- A piping bag with fine nozzles for icing and decorating sweets.
- Cookie cutters.

Cooking Sugar

The physical properties of sugar syrup change as it reaches different temperatures. To make a range of sweets, you will need to become familiar with the different stages of cooking sugar. Please be aware that the temperatures involved are high and hot sugar retains its heat for a long time. Care should always be taken to prevent accidents and injuries, so avoid contact with the skin. However delicious the bubbling mixture looks, do not be tempted to try it – the injury will be severe.

For accurate results in cooking sugar, a thermometer is a must. It is a good idea to test your thermometer by placing it in a pan of water and checking the boiling point. You should, of course, see the water boil at 100°C (212°F).

Thread stage 110°–112°C (230–235°F)
This stage is used for making sugar syrups. It gives a nice, thick, pourable syrup that is great for ice creams or for sauces in desserts.

Soft Ball stage 115°–117°C (240–245°F)
As the name suggests, sugar at this temperature cools to form a soft, pliable ball. You will become familiar with this stage in

cooking fudges and fondants. Once the temperature is reached, remove from the heat immediately to ensure it does not become too hard.

Firm Ball stage 118°–121°C (245–250°F)

This stage is used to create those lovely caramel toffees that are hard in the first instance but become wonderfully gloopy and sticky as you eat. As you test it, it will form a little ball that is less malleable than at the soft ball stage.

Hard Ball stage 121°–123°C (250–265°F)

A noticeably hard ball forms when a teaspoon of the mixture is placed on a cold saucer. The mixture will form solid 'stalactites' as it drips from the spoon. It is still pliable, but it is more difficult to alter its shape. This is the temperature needed to make nougat and rock candy.

Soft Crack stage 131°–143°C (270–290°F)

The mixture is now on the verge of becoming brittle. When cool, drips from the spoon will bend slightly and then break. This is the stage needed for butterscotch and some boiled sweets.

Hard Crack stage 148°–154°C (300–310°F)

At these temperatures, the sugar, once cooled, will be brittle and snap. It is imperative that you take great care when handling pans of sugar at these temperatures and do not handle tested balls until they have cooled. You'll need to reach the hard crack stage when making peanut brittle and most boiled sweets.

Caramels

Temperatures greater than the hard crack stage will provide you with caramelised sugar. Be aware of the fact that boiling sugar remains hot for a long time after you remove it from the heat, so do not be tempted to dip your finger in the mixture.

The stages of caramelisation arrive quickly, so as soon as the mixture changes colour it is best to remove it from the heat as the sugar continues to cook after this.

Clear Liquid stage 160°C (320°F)
This is the point at which your colourless sugar syrup begins to change colour. For delicate flavours, remove from the heat now.

Brown Liquid stage 170°C (338°F)
The syrup is richer and has a stronger flavour. It is a deep brown colour. Take care as the next phase is the burnt sugar stage, which has a bitter taste, and can arrive quicker than you expect, usually after around 175°C (347°F).

Chapter One
Making Fudge

Techniques for Making Fudge

The Pan

The most important piece of equipment for making successful fudge is the pan. It should be as sturdy as you can afford, especially around the handle area as the very last thing you want is boiling sugar flying across the room because it fell off. The key is to have a pan that distributes the heat evenly across the base. The only way you'll know if it does this is to use it a few times. Pans that heat unevenly will result in some of your ingredients being raw and some being burnt, and you being extremely unhappy. The pan needs to be smooth in order to ensure your fudge forms the smallest crystals possible.

Thermometer

A thermometer is the only way to get a precise temperature and a must for beginners. Preserving thermometers are relatively inexpensive (between £7 and £25) and, for me, took the stress out of making fudge in the beginning. You will spend at least £5 on your ingredients and it can get somewhat frustrating on the purse if you guess and do not get the desired results straight away. Of course, my dear old Grandma wouldn't have bothered with one, and there will be thousands of people up and down the country that will roll their eyes at using a thermometer, but in the beginning I wouldn't even try to make fudge without one. As you get used to the process and your equipment, you will start to see when things are ready, and testing using a cold saucer will become your desired method. The bragging rights for getting to this stage are particularly exciting!

Spoon

A long-handled spoon really helps avoid any sugar injuries, as you'll do a lot of stirring in the process. If you don't have one and aren't confident (or are a complete klutz, like me), wear clean gardening gloves to ensure your digits remain intact.

You

The key to making fudge is to understand that the main piece of equipment is you and your environment. Every pan, kitchen and cooker is different.

You have to find your own method, and as long as you understand the transformation that your ingredients undergo in the pan, you will be able to adjust any recipe.

The Perfect Fudge

This is a matter of taste, but most people like a smooth, grain-free texture. To achieve this, diligence is needed in ensuring the sugar crystals remain as small as possible.

Stage one *dissolving sugar*

Basic chemistry classes will tell you that sugar dissolves quicker in warm liquids. Gently heating the sugar accelerates the process. The liquid you use in your recipe, be it milk, evaporated milk or cream, can only dissolve so much sugar without it becoming saturated. This means it has taken as much of the sugar molecules as it can hold. As the temperature rises, the liquid can hold more dissolved sugar than it could at lower temperatures. Heating the liquid gently not only ensures the liquid can hold more dissolved sugar, but the end result will be smoother.

Stage two *boiling*

Milk boils at a similar temperature to water (i.e. 100°C/212°F) but dissolving the sugar in it alters the boiling point. The more sugar dissolved in the liquid, the higher the boiling point. This is why some days your fudge will be ready at 114°C, some days it will take up to 118°C. It's all due to the amount of sugar in your liquid. This can vary just by a slip of the hand as you pour the sugar into the pan, but understanding this point will allow you to make judgements as you make your own batches.

Stage Three *cooling down*
When saturated solutions cool down, crystals are formed. For good fudge, you want very small crystals to form uniformly, to get that nice smooth texture. Annoyingly, the sugar will crystallise on imperfections in the pan, hence the need to have a good clean surface to work in. Similarly, as your sugar solution boils, crystals may form on the sides of the pan, encouraging crystallisation, so you may need to wash the sides of the pan with a pastry brush dipped in water during the cooking process.

Stage four *stirring*
As the mixture cools, the tendency for crystals to form increases. This process ensures your final product has a firm texture. The best way to make sure that your fudge has small crystals is to stir the mixture vigorously after it cools slightly. The action of stirring both encourages many crystals to form, but as they are constantly moving they do not form large enough to be noticeable. You will also notice that the glossy mixture turns matt in texture.

Troubleshooting
My fudge did not set!
Your mixture did not reach the correct temperature. The mixture needs to reach the boiling point for a sugar solution in order to set. If you are using a recipe from the internet, it may be you had too much liquid in the mix!

My fudge is too solid!
Your mixture got too hot. The temperature needed for fudge is known

as the soft ball stage. As you heat sugar to higher temperatures, you will reach the cracking stage. This is a bit unkind on the teeth!

My fudge is solid, but turns to dust!

The sugar crystals have formed too large. This can be due to leaving the mixture to cool, allowing the crystals to form, or to using a pan with a rough surface. It can also happen if the mixture is not stirred vigorously enough during cooling.

Plain Fudge

This is the basic recipe that will see you through many of the variations in this book. It is a good idea to master this a few times before you commit yourself to making anything more exotic. If you've never made fudge before, it's best to buy enough ingredients to make three batches and to be prepared to write off your first one as a disaster as there are so many factors that can conspire against you. Once you've got it, it's as easy as this...

MAKES 2 GIFTS

300g caster sugar
300ml double cream
75g salted butter

---

1. Grease a 20cm square tray and line with foil. Place the sugar and cream into your chosen pan over a very low heat.

2. Slowly melt the sugar, stirring gently with a tablespoon. It is ready when the grains of sugar no longer appear on the back of the spoon. This can take up to 10 minutes – your fudge will be smoother if you melt the sugar slowly.

3. When the sugar has melted, bring the mixture to the boil slowly. When the mixture is bubbling (on the lowest possible heat), put the lid on and leave it to boil for 3 minutes.

4. Remove the lid and place your thermometer into the mix. Gradually increase the temperature (over 10 minutes or so) until you reach 116°C (240.8°F). Remove the pan from the heat.

5. Add the butter to the pan and allow to melt, stirring gently. Once the butter is fully combined, pour the mixture into the tray and leave to cool. Once cooled, place in a fridge for at least 4 hours before removing from the tray and cutting into delicious bite-sized chunks.

6. Store in an airtight container in a cool, dark place. It should keep for about 10–12 days.

Chocolate Fudge

This can be altered to cater to all tastes. If you like white chocolate, simply use this in the recipe (but use 75g rather than 100g as it will be extremely sweet!), or if you prefer dark chocolate, use the best quality with the highest cocoa solids you can find. A little of this fudge really does go a long way, but this recipe will make enough for 3 small or 2 generous portions.

MAKES 2 GIFTS

300g golden caster sugar
300ml double cream
100g chocolate of
your choice
70g salted butter

---

1. Grease a 20cm square tray and line with foil or silicone paper. Follow the instructions in the Plain Fudge recipe (page 11) up to stage 4.

2. Melt the chocolate in a separate bowl over a pan of boiling water.

3. Add the butter to the pan, along with the chocolate. Stir gently until the butter has melted and the mixture is glossy.

4. Pour the mixture into the greased tray and leave to cool. Once at room temperature, refrigerate for at least 4 hours, before chopping into 2½cm cubes.

5. Store in an airtight container in a cool, dark place. It should keep for about 10–12 days.

Vanilla Fudge

To make a vanilla fudge, simply add 5 drops of vanilla extract before stage 2. You can also scrape the seeds from a vanilla pod and add them at the same time.

Cappuccino Fudge

Delicious served with a tall latte, or cut into small cubes and cooked in a coffee cake, this fudge is a great gift for coffee lovers. It is made in two stages, to mimic the white foam on top of a cappuccino and looks rather lovely presented in a large coffee cup. For those who prefer a stronger coffee flavour, use 2 shots of espresso and reduce the amount of cream to 240ml.

MAKES 2 GIFTS

For the coffee layer
300g demerara sugar
270ml double cream
1 shot of espresso or 1 teaspoon instant coffe dissolved in 30ml almost boiling water
75g salted butter

---

1. Grease a 20cm square tray and line with foil.

2. Add the sugar, cream and coffee to the pan. Now follow the Plain Fudge recipe (page 11), stages 2–4.

3. Add the butter to the pan and allow it to melt, stirring gently. Once the butter is fully combined, your fudge is ready.

4. Pour the fudge into your tray, leaving an 8mm gap at the top for your milky layer.

For the milky layer
100g white marshmallows
100g white chocolate
50g butter

---

5. Place all the ingredients in a bowl over a pan of gently simmering water until fully melted, stirring gently.

6. When it has formed a thick, glossy liquid, pour over the cooled coffee fudge and leave to cool.

7. When set, cut into 2½cm cubes and present in a large coffee cup.

8. Store in an airtight container in a cool, dark place. It should keep for about 10–12 days.

Raspberry and White Chocolate Fudge

An elegant fudge that looks glorious in red and cream packaging, this also makes a wonderful wedding reception favour. It is best to use dried raspberries, not only for flavour, but to ensure your fudge sets, as the higher quantity of liquid in fresh raspberries may make it too squidgy. For pink-themed weddings, why not add a couple of drops of pink food colouring to give it an extra zing!

MAKES 2 GIFTS

300g white caster sugar
300ml double cream
75g salted butter, cut into chunks
100g white chocolate, melted
100g dried raspberries

1. Grease a 20cm square tray and line with foil.

2. Add the caster sugar and cream to the pan and follow the instructions in the Plain Fudge recipe (page 11), stages 2–4. If you wish to make a pink version, add a few drops of food colouring after the cream.

3. Add the butter and melted chocolate to the pan, stirring gently until the butter is fully melted and both are combined fully. This will take around 3–5 minutes.

4. Add the dried raspberries to the pan and stir. Pour the mixture into the tray and leave to cool. Refrigerate for at least 4 hours and then cut into chunks.

5. Store in an airtight container in a cool, dark place. It should keep for about 10–12 days.

6. For a wedding or party treat, stab the fudge pieces onto skewers and place 2 pieces per person on a plate in the centre of the table. Make a raspberry dip by placing 100g frozen raspberries in a blender with 1 tablespoon caster sugar and blend until smooth. Push the mixture through a sieve to remove any seeds. Keep the dip in the fridge until you are ready to use it.

CHRISTMAS FUDGE

A delicious treat any time of year, this recipe uses seasonal ingredients that will make a perfect Christmas present for even the most difficult-to-buy-for friends and family. You can make this using any of your favourite nuts or dried fruit, though cranberries and pecans work really well with good quality dark chocolate.

MAKES 2 GIFTS

300g golden caster sugar
300ml double cream
100g dark chocolate
70g salted butter
1 teaspoon allspice
50g cranberries
50g pecan nuts, chopped
50g glacé cherries, chopped
50g white chocolate (optional)

---

1. Grease a 20cm square tray and line with foil. Follow the instructions in the Plain Fudge recipe (page 11) up to stage 4.

2. Melt the dark chocolate in a separate bowl over a pan of boiling water.

3. Add the butter to the pan, along with the chocolate and allspice. Stir gently until the butter has melted and the mixture is glossy.

4. Quickly add most of the cranberries, pecans and cherries (retaining some for decoration) to the mixture. Stir through the mixture so they are evenly distributed and pour into the tray.

5. While the mixture is still hot, sprinkle the remaining nuts on top for decoration and leave to cool.

6. Refrigerate for at least 4 hours before removing from the tray and chopping into 2½cm pieces and placing into a decorative box.

7. Store in an airtight container in a cool, dark place. It should keep for about 10–12 days.

8. For an extra festive look, melt the white chocolate in a bowl over a pan of boiling water and drizzle over the top of your cubes.

Coconut Fudge

A Caribbean treat, perfect with a Malibu cocktail and a sandy beach! This recipe uses a mixture of coconut milk and cream and is wonderfully rich. For fans of the chocolate bar Bounty, coat the fudge in chocolate and see how quickly the batch disappears!

MAKES 2 GIFTS

300g white caster sugar
150ml double cream
150ml coconut milk
75g creamed coconut
40g desiccated coconut for decoration

---

1. Grease a 20cm square tray and line with foil.

2. Add the sugar, cream and coconut milk to the pan and follow the Plain Fudge recipe (page 11), stages 2–4.

3. Remove the pan from the heat and add the creamed coconut. Stir until fully melted and combined.

4. Pour into the tray and sprinkle with desiccated coconut before the mixture sets fully. Refrigerate for 4 hours before cutting into generous chunks.

5. Store in an airtight container in a cool, dark place. It should keep for about 10–12 days.

LEMON DRIZZLE FUDGE

A refreshing fudge that is perfect for a summer's day. It goes brilliantly with the Limoncello recipe (page 140) and is another elegant idea for a wedding favour or thank you gift.

MAKES 2 GIFTS

300g white caster sugar
300ml double cream
Juice of 2 lemons
75g butter
Zest of 1 lemon

1. Grease a 20cm square tray and line with foil.

2. Add the sugar, cream and lemon juice to the pan and follow the Plain Fudge recipe (page 11), stages 2–4.

3. Remove from the heat and add the butter and lemon zest. Stir quickly until the butter is incorporated.

4. Pour into a tray and refrigerate for 4 hours before cutting into chunks.

5. You can make this look even more special by making a lemon-flavoured icing and drizzling it over the top. See the Royal Icing recipe (page 116), whisking 1 teaspoon fresh lemon juice per 100g sugar into the egg whites.

6. Store in an airtight container in a cool, dark place. It should keep for about 10–12 days.

Rum and Raisin Fudge

This is a firm favourite with many people and makes a lovely addition to rum and raisin ice cream when chopped up small.

MAKES 2 GIFTS

100g raisins
40ml dark rum
300g soft brown sugar
300ml evaporated milk
75g butter

---

1. Place the raisins in a bowl and cover with the rum. Leave to soak for 2 hours (or overnight for fat juicy raisins!).

2. Grease a 20cm square tray and line with foil.

3. Add the sugar and evaporated milk to a pan and follow the Plain Fudge recipe (page 11), stages 2–4.

4. Remove from the heat and add the butter. Stir in the rum and raisins until fully incorporated.

5. Pour into the tray and leave to cool before refrigerating for 4 hours. Chop into 2½cm cubes.

6. Store in an airtight container in a cool, dark place. It should keep for about 10–12 days.

IRISH CREAM FUDGE

This is perfect for fans of Irish Cream liqueur, and makes a great gift when coupled with a little bottle of something special...

MAKES 2 GIFTS

300g golden caster sugar
300ml double cream
50ml Irish Cream liqueur
75g butter
50g white chocolate to drizzle (optional)

1. Grease a 20cm square tray and line with foil.

2. Add the ingredients to the pan and follow the Plain Fudge recipe (page 11), up to stage 5.

3. For an extra dimension, drizzle with lots of melted white chocolate while still in the tray and leave to cool before chopping into 2½cm cubes.

4. Store in an airtight container in a cool, dark place. It should keep for about 10–12 days.

STRAWBERRY FUDGE

A delicious summery fudge that goes wonderfully with a glass of champagne. A brilliant addition to a garden party!

MAKES 2 GIFTS

300g white caster sugar
300ml double cream
200g fresh strawberries, chopped
75g butter

---

1. Grease a 20cm square tray and line with foil.

2. Add the sugar and cream together in a pan and slowly bring up to 112°C (238°F).

3. Add the chopped strawberries, put the lid on and boil for 3 minutes.

4. Remove the lid and boil until the temperature reaches 117°C (242°F).

5. Remove from the heat, add the butter and stir until melted.

6. Pour the mixture into the tray and leave to cool before cutting into chunks.

7. Store in an airtight container in a cool, dark place. It should keep for about 10–12 days.

Chapter Two
Making Caramel and Toffee

Techniques for Making Toffee and Caramel

The rich flavour we know and love in toffee and caramel comes from cooking the sugar for longer than in making fudge. The sugar needs to be cooked slowly and for a long time to ensure it changes as you would expect. Caramelisation of sugar is a complex process, which involves a number of chemical processes. The key things to remember here are:

- Cooking the sugar slowly for a long time gives a good depth of flavour and a deeper colour.

- Cooking quickly will give lighter colours, but it is possible to cook the sugar too quickly so that it scorches and gives a burnt flavour.

- Cooking slowly means melting the sugar slowly and increasing the temperature gradually. Putting the pan over a high heat will not give you the desired result.

For chewy toffee you will need to cook the sugar until it reaches the firm ball stage, which is between 118°C and 121°C (245–250°F). Usually you should aim for 120°C (248°F) to get a suitable firm toffee that won't rip your teeth out. For caramel that can be used in cooking, you will need to use more liquid and cook for less time. So let's get on with it, shall we?

LUXURY CHEWY TOFFEE

An extremely creamy and moreish caramel that tastes as good if not better than the premium brand of caramel toffee that can be purchased in the shops. It can be rolled into small balls if you like and dipped in melted chocolate.

MAKES 1 GIFT

240ml double cream
75g butter
60g golden syrup
60ml milk
200g soft brown sugar
½–1 teaspoon vanilla extract

1. Grease and line a 20cm square, shallow baking tin.

2. Put the cream and butter in a pan over a low heat until the butter has thoroughly melted into the cream. Remove from the heat and set aside.

3. Put the syrup, milk and sugar in a sturdy pan over a low heat and stir gently until all the sugar has dissolved.

4. Bring the mixture to the boil and continue to boil for 3 minutes. Then remove from the heat.

5. Slowly pour the cream mixture into the syrup, taking care as it will bubble up. Stir a couple of times to combine then return to the heat. Bring to the boil again and use a thermometer to measure the temperature. When it has reached 120°C (250°F) remove from the heat and stir in the vanilla.

6. Pour into the prepared tin and allow to cool. When cool, place in the fridge.

7. When chilled after about 1 hour, turn onto a clean chopping board. Use a hot knife to cut the caramel into small cubes of whatever size you wish.

8. Wrap individually or place in layers separated between silicone paper to stop it from sticking together too much. It will keep for 12–15 days in an airtight container.

Soft Caramel

This recipe is quick and easy and makes a much softer caramel that is ideal for fillings and toppings for biscuits such as Millionaire Shortbread.

MAKES 700G

400g can condensed milk
150g butter
150g soft brown sugar

---

1. Put all the ingredients in a sturdy pan and heat gently over a low heat, stirring until all the sugar has dissolved.

2. Bring to the boil and continue to boil for about 3 minutes or until thickened and smooth.

3. This can be used in your Millionaire Shortbread immediately or cooled and added to other recipes.

Useful Tip
This recipe is also good for dipping apples into to make Caramel Apples. Dip them whilst the caramel is warm and then roll the apple into nuts, chocolate chips or toffee pieces and leave to cool for a delicious treat. Turn to page 30 for more details.

Very Easy Caramel

This makes a tasty caramel without using sugar or condensed milk. It isn't as luxurious as the first recipe though. It is useful for making toffee apples as it is quick and there is no need to dissolve any sugar.

MAKES 1 GIFT

85g butter
140g golden syrup
150g honey

---

1. Grease and line an 18cm square tin.

2. Put all the ingredients together in the pan and heat slowly to boiling point, stirring to incorporate the butter.

3. Continue boiling until the mixture reaches 120°C (250°F).

4. Remove from the heat and beat well with a wooden spoon for 5 minutes or until the mixture is opaque.

5. Pour the mixture into the prepared tin and allow to cool.

6. Whilst still warm, but not hot, cut into squares with a hot knife and leave it to go completely cold.

7. Wrap individually or place in layers separated between silicone paper to stop it from sticking together too much. It will keep for 12 days in an airtight container.

Variations

Add 50g glacé cherries, chopped.
Add 80g mixed raisins and almonds.
Replace 20g golden syrup with 20g treacle.
Add 2 teaspoons vanilla extract.
Add 1 teaspoon peppermint natural flavour.

These variations must be added after the firm ball stage is reached and stirred in prior to beating, i.e. between steps 3 and 4.

APPLE CARAMELS

These are extremely moreish and are a lovely autumnal sweet that will sure to be a favourite. For a boozy version, use good quality cider instead of apple juice, or for a little kick, use half and half!

MAKES 2 GIFTS

450ml good quality apple juice
350g golden caster sugar
2 tablespoons golden syrup
1 teaspoon cinnamon
250ml double cream
100g butter, cut into cubes

---

1. Line a 20cm square tin with silicone paper and grease with butter.

2. Pour the apple juice into a solid pan and bring to the boil. Then turn down the heat and reduce the juice by half.

3. Add the sugar, syrup, cinnamon and cream. Slowly increase the heat until the temperature reaches 112°C (234°F) and the sugar has dissolved and you have a glossy liquid with no grains.

4. Add the cubed butter and stir slowly, until the butter melts into the liquid. Gradually increase the heat until the temperature reaches 120°C (248°F).

5. Remove from the heat and leave to stand for 30 seconds before pouring the mixture into your tin. Leave to cool and refrigerate overnight.

6. Using a large knife, cut into squares and wrap in small squares of greaseproof paper. Store in an airtight container. It will keep for 12 days.

BONFIRE TOFFEE

Bonfire night would not be the same without the luscious, creamy dark toffee. The burnt flavour is achieved through the use of black treacle in the recipe, which is made from the residue left after sugar is refined. It is not as sweet as golden syrup, and has a slightly bitter taste, which works wonders in this recipe, which we've used and perfected every year since we can remember.

This recipe makes about 400g. It is a creamier version of the original toffee which doesn't contain butter.

MAKES 2 GIFTS

300g soft brown sugar
100g butter (use salted for the best flavour)
2 tablespoons golden syrup
2 tablespoons black treacle
4 tablespoons water

---

1. Line an 18cm square, shallow tin with baking paper.

2. Put all the ingredients together in a sturdy pan.

3. Heat slowly over a low heat, stirring continuously until the butter melts and the sugar dissolves.

4. Raise the heat and bring to the boil, stirring occasionally.

5. When boiling vigorously start to measure the temperature. It should take about 12 minutes to reach 140°C. As soon as this temperature is reached remove from the heat and pour into the prepared tin.

6. Allow it to go completely cold, then turn out onto some greaseproof paper and break up with a rolling pin or a good toffee hammer.

7. Store in an airtight container lined with greaseproof paper. It will keep for 15 days.

TOFFEE POPCORN

This toffee popcorn is a favourite of our friend James, who would eat it until it came out of his ears, but thankfully it runs out before that happens. A bag of this is the perfect gift accompaniment to a pair of cinema tickets, which is a great present for teenagers.

MAKES 2 GIFTS

60g salted butter
75g soft brown sugar
2 tablespoons honey or golden syrup
150g popcorn, popped

---

1. Melt the butter in a pan over a low heat. Add the sugar and honey or syrup and melt slowly, increasing the heat until bubbling.

2. Place the popcorn in a large bowl and pour the toffee sauce over. Stir with a wooden spoon to coat evenly.

3. Leave to cool and package in large cellophane bags tied with ribbon. Alternatively, store in an airtight container and it will keep for 4–5 days.

Chapter Three
Chocolate

Heating and Melting Chocolate

Chocolate is a delicate ingredient to work with and it requires careful handling when being cooked or heated. Never melt chocolate directly in a pan on its own. Always use either a double boiler or a heatproof glass bowl over a pan of simmering water. Or use a microwave. When melting chocolate never allow it to come into contact with water or steam as it will become grainy and stiff and unmeltable.

Hob method
For approximately 150g chocolate

1. Break up or chop the chocolate into small pieces and place in a glass bowl.

2. Pour hot water into a pan and place the bowl inside the pan, ensuring the bottom of the bowl does not make contact with the water.

3. Bring the water to simmering and as the chocolate melts move it gently around with a spatula rather than stirring, as this can cause the chocolate to split.

4. When fully melted, turn off the heat and the chocolate will remain fluid for about 25–30 minutes.

Microwave method
For approximately 150g chocolate

1. Break up or chop the chocolate and place in a microwavable bowl.

2. Use a medium to high setting and place the bowl in the machine. Cook for 1 minute then check. Move the chocolate around the bowl with a spatula, rather than stirring.

3. Cook for 1 more minute and it should be fully melted and ready to use.

Types of Chocolate

Dark chocolate
This comes in varieties depending on the cocoa solid content. Anything between 35% and 85% cocoa solids is classed as dark chocolate. The more cocoa solids the chocolate contains, the less cocoa butter content. This means that the chocolate is more brittle and takes longer to melt. It also contains less sugar. If your recipe requires dark chocolate, use one that has between 55% and 70% cocoa solids.

Milk chocolate
This is easier to melt as it has a higher cocoa butter content. It is sweeter than dark chocolate so take this into consideration when using it in your recipes. In baking it is better used in combination with dark chocolate as this gives a better flavour.

White chocolate
This contains only cocoa butter and no solids. It has a rich creamy flavour and can, if overused in a recipe, become too sweet and sickly.

Enrobing Fruits with Chocolate

Use only absolutely perfect fresh fruit and it must be washed and dried well. It doesn't keep for much longer than a week so ensure any recipients realise the short shelf life of their gift. Dried fruit is also good to coat in chocolate and it keeps longer than fresh.

Coating the Fruit

100g chocolate coats about 20–25 pieces of fruit depending on the size.

1. Have a tray lined with baking or silicone paper ready to stand the chocolates on. I like to chill my tray in the freezer first as it helps set the chocolate quicker. Also have lots of cocktail sticks to hand to dip your fruit with.

2. Melt the chocolate as described on page 35. Having two types of melted chocolate ready, dark and white for example, enables you to either dip twice for a double layer or half coat one side in white and the other in dark.

   If you wish to double coat, dip the fruit in one type of chocolate then allow it to set before dipping in the second coat.

   If doing half and half, dip one side in one type then allow it to set before dipping the other side in the contrasting chocolate.

3. To add another dimension to the dipped fruits, try dipping in chopped or ground nuts before allowing the chocolate to set.

Useful Tip

If you want to dip small items of dried fruit such as raisins or sultanas, thread 2 or 3 onto the cocktail stick before dipping for best results.

SPECIAL CHOCOLATE APPLE SLICES

These look as impressive as they taste, and are a wonderful gift for fans of apple. This is also a great way of making your home-grown apples last a little longer, as enrobing them in chocolate will preserve the apple for a week. The key to this is to have a good space to work on, so clear off a table and give yourself room for all the different bowls and racks!

MAKES ONE DECENT-SIZED GIFT

100g milk chocolate
100g white chocolate
2 apples of your choice
(the larger the better)
50g nuts, chopped
50g desiccated coconut
Hundreds & thousands

---

1. Melt the chocolate separately in bowls over pans of gently simmering water, as described on page 35.

2. Peel and core the apples, and cut into 1cm slices. Place a sheet of silicone paper on a tray and lay the slices on top. Pat them dry.

3. Place your nuts, coconut and hundreds and thousands into separate bowls for ease of dipping.

4. Dip the slice of apple fully into the chocolate and place on the silicone paper. Sprinkle a teaspoon of desiccated coconut over the slice while the chocolate is still warm so it adheres.

5. Repeat with another slice and sprinkle with nuts, then again with another slice and sprinkle with hundreds and thousands, until all slices are covered. Leave to cool in the refrigerator before packaging. They will keep for 1 week.

Boozy Enrobed Fruit

You'll find these in smart chocolateries for rather an alarming amount of money, but they are so easy to make, especially if you already have a cheeky bottle of something in the cupboard.

MAKES ONE GIFT

100g dried fruit
50ml liqueur or spirit
100g chocolate

---

1. Simply take the dried fruit of your choice and soak overnight in 50ml of the liqueur or spirit of your choice in a covered bowl.

2. Remove the fruit from the bowl and leave it to dry out a little on a baking tray.

3. Enrobe the fruit in chocolate as described above, double coating for extra decadence. You'll be asked to make these again and again! They will keep for 1 week.

Variations
- Dried strawberries soaked in crème de fraise and dipped in white chocolate.
- Dried mango pieces in brandy, dipped in dark chocolate.
- Dried cranberries in brandy, dipped in white and milk chocolate.
- Dried pineapple in Calvados, dipped in milk chocolate.

Using Chocolate Moulds

Why not try making your own Easter eggs, chocolate teddies, Christmas snowmen or Father Christmases? Moulds of many shapes can be purchased from chocolate-making websites and also from craft shops, such as The Range and Hobbycraft (see p.146).

The moulds usually come in two halves so you can melt your chocolate, pour it into each half of the mould and move it around so the chocolate coats the entire surface of the mould. Leave it to set in the fridge and repeat this process until you get the desired thickness of the shell, depending on how generous you are feeling!

Chill in the fridge for an hour then carefully remove the chocolate from the mould and fill with other goodies if it is for Easter or simply join the two halves.

To 'glue' the moulded chocolate, place the two halves together and use a hot knife to close the seam. Simply lay it flat against the seam and leave to cool. Do not leave the knife against the chocolate for too long as your shape may melt and lose definition. The best way to heat your knife is with a flame rather than in hot water, so ensure you use a plastic-handled blade as you heat it briefly in the gas flame. If you prefer to use hot water, ensure you dry the knife before using.

CHOCOLATE TRUFFLES

These have got to be the ultimate chocolate luxury, and are definitely my favourite. The creamy, smooth combination of chocolate and double cream is sublime. They are also much easier to make than you think, if a little messy!

There are two stages to making truffles: first, making the ganache centre and second, dipping in various coatings.

What is ganache?

This is the combination of melted chocolate and double cream to make a firm yet workable centre to your truffles. The ganache is made first and allowed to firm up in the fridge for a few hours before finishing your truffles.

Turn the page to discover how to make it...

GANACHE

MAKES ABOUT 25 GOOD-SIZED TRUFFLES

200g dark chocolate (60–70% cocoa solids gives the best results)
180ml double cream
20g unsalted butter

---

1. Chop the chocolate into small pieces.

2. Place the cream and butter in a bowl over a pan of simmering water. When the butter has melted, stir gently into the cream and add the chocolate. Don't stir until the chocolate looks as though it is melting.

3. Gently move the chocolate into the cream now and again.

4. When the chocolate has melted, remove from the heat and stir slowly, but make sure the chocolate and cream are thoroughly combined.

5. If you wish to make additions to your ganache, stir these in as soon as the chocolate and cream are combined and still warm.

6. Leave to cool for 5 minutes then place in the fridge for at least 1 hour to firm up.

Additions

- 2 tablespoons brandy or rum.
- 1 tablespoon Tia Maria or other flavoured liqueur.
- Dried fruits – these may be soaked in brandy or rum beforehand for a few hours. Chop cherries or large pieces of fruit before adding to the ganache mixture.
- 2–3 tablespoons chopped nuts.
- 2 tablespoons desiccated or freshly grated coconut.
- 1 tablespoon Limoncello, 1 tablespoon of lemon juice and meringue pieces for a lemon meringue pie truffle.
- 3 drops peppermint essence.

Finishing the Truffles

1. Keep the room and yourself as cool as possible as the ganache soon melts. I always run my wrists under the cold tap for a minute or so prior to making the truffles. It seems to keep my hands cool longer.

2. Have some small bowls ready containing ground or chopped nuts, desiccated coconut, cocoa powder, icing sugar or melted chocolate to dip your truffles into.

3. When the mixture is cold and firm, use a melon baller or two teaspoons to form the ganache into small balls.

4. Using a cocktail stick, stab the ganache balls and dip into the coatings. If you dip into chocolate, you may wish to stab the other end of the cocktail stick into an apple or orange to ensure the chocolate dries evenly around the ball.

5. Put each truffle as you finish it into a small petit four-sized paper case. These are readily available in the bakery section of the supermarket.

6. As soon as they are finished, place in the containers you are using to present them and place in the fridge.

7. They will keep best in a cold place and will stay fresh for 2 weeks. Make them just before you present them and add a label to say how long they should be kept for.

Chocolate Pralines

This marvellous confectionery is a mixture of hazelnuts, caramelised sugar and chocolate. The praline is made separately (see p. 47) so it can be used on its own to decorate other sweet treats or mixed with chocolate to make the chocolate variety (see p. 48).

Chocolate Slabs

These are a very easy but impressive way to present your chocolate gifts. You can tailor your slabs to your recipient, using their favourite ingredients.

It is simply a matter of melting the chocolate and pouring it carefully onto a sheet of silicone paper. To make it easier and also to make the slab deeper and an interesting shape, use a shaped cutter as a mould. If you want to make it into a rectangle, use a butter container, the rigid plastic type. Cut the base away neatly and use this to shape your slab. You can also buy chocolate moulds and shapes from specialist websites (see p. 146).

Have ready a selection of dried or crystallised fruits, nuts chopped or whole. Whatever your recipient would like from crushed Maltesers® to hundreds and thousands – be creative.

MAKING A SMALL CHOCOLATE SLAB*

200g chocolate (use a mixture if required up to a total of 200g)
50g fruit or nuts of your choice
50g sweets of your choice

---

* To make a family sized bar, use a total of 800g chocolate and 150g additions (sweets, nuts, fruit, etc). You can use a shallow cake tin or baking tray to set the chocolate in, just be sure to line it with silicone paper.

1. Melt your chocolate.

2. Either pour the chocolate straight onto the silicone paper to make a thin slab or into your chosen shape.

3. Allow it to set for a few minutes then press the decorations gently into the chocolate.

4. Leave it to set in the fridge when cool. When the slabs have set, wrap them in cellophane or whatever way you wish to present them.

5. Store in an airtight container in a cool dark place.

Variations
- After the chocolate has set, melt another batch of either the same type of chocolate or a contrasting one and pour this over to give a two-layered effect. You can buy coloured chocolate drops, either online or in craft shops, which makes a fantastic contrasting chocolate for slabs.
- If you don't wish to add fruit and nuts to the slab, try drizzling contrasting chocolate over the set slab for an artistic finish.
- Make a slab of milk chocolate and when it is set break into small pieces. Place in a cellophane bag and tie with ribbon for a quick gift.
- Make a slab of dark or white chocolate and sprinkle milk chocolate over the top as it sets. You can vary this to suit your taste.

MAKING PRALINE

150g whole hazelnuts, skinned
150g caster sugar

1. Cover a baking sheet with silicone paper.

2. Place the nuts on a roasting tray and roast for 5–10 minutes at 180°C/Gas 4.

3. Put the sugar in a sturdy pan and dissolve over a medium heat. Do not stir, just move the pan around so the sugar dissolves evenly.

4. Allow the sugar to turn golden and add the nuts. Stir gently to coat the nuts thoroughly with the caramel.

5. Pour onto the silicone paper and allow to cool and harden completely.

6. When hard, mix to a smooth consistency in a food processor. It may be left as coarse as you wish, but traditional chocolate praline uses a smooth nut mixture. This can be used as it is to flavour cakes and fillings or to decorate sweets and cakes.

7. Store in a lidded container in a cool dark place. It should keep for 21 days.

MAKING CHOCOLATE PRALINE

300g good quality chocolate
300g praline

---

1. Melt the chocolate and stir the praline gently into the melted chocolate until well combined.

2. Spoon into paper cases or allow to set in a square baking tin then cut into delicious pieces. Wrap using tongs as they melt very quickly if handled.

3. Store in a lidded container in a cool dark place. It should keep for 14 days.

Gianduja

This is a form of chocolate praline. It contains 30% extra smooth praline to 70% chocolate.

MAKES 20 PIECES

225g good quality
milk chocolate
100g praline (see p. 47)

---

1. Blend the praline in a processor until it is a smooth paste.

2. Melt the chocolate. Just before it sets combine with the praline, mixing together with a spatula – don't beat, just mix thoroughly.

3. Spread evenly into a shallow tray. Allow to set completely, preferably in a fridge set to a medium setting, not too cold.

4. Cut into small bricks and wrap in special chocolate foil wrappers*.

5. Store in a lidded container in a cool dark place. Keeps for 2 weeks.

* These are available from confectionery supply shops. Alternatively, use some silicone paper and wrap them like small presents, keeping them closed with a sticky label. These are a decadent and impressive gift.

CHOCOLATE PUDDING TREATS

My Mum and I used to make these with any leftover Christmas pudding and Christmas cake. We liked to add extra glacé cherries but you can leave these out if you wish.

MAKES ABOUT 20–25

400g Christmas pudding and/or cake
200g dark chocolate
10g butter
50g glacé cherries, chopped (optional)
100g white chocolate
5 or 6 glacé cherries, cut into quarters

---

1. Put the pudding and cake if using in a mixing bowl and crumble with your fingers until it is quite fine.

2. Melt the chocolate in a bowl with the butter.

3. Stir the cherries if using into the pudding. Stir the chocolate into the pudding and mix well to combine.

4 Form into small balls of the desired size and place in the petit four cases.

5. Melt the white chocolate and spoon a little on the top of each pudding. Top with a piece of cherry.

6. To add a little extra luxury, drizzle 4–5 tablespoons rum or brandy over the pudding and/or cake mixture before mixing with the chocolate.

7. Store in an airtight container. They will keep for 7 days.

CHOCOLATE CAKE TRUFFLES

These are quick, easy and very delicious. They make a great alternative to a chocolate cake for a birthday party, or for grown-up parties*, try placing them on skewers and tie a ribbon round to turn into a 'cake pop'.

Makes about 15

150g chocolate cake, remove any filling and break into crumbs so there are no large pieces (the cake can even be a little stale)
30g icing sugar
20g cocoa powder
25g butter
3 tablespoons rum
150g dark chocolate

---

1. Cover a baking tray with silicone paper.

2. Put the cake crumbs in a mixing bowl.

3. Sift the icing sugar and cocoa powder together then stir into the cake crumbs.

4. Melt the butter gently in a pan and pour into the cake mixture. Before stirring in the butter, sprinkle in the rum and then stir well with a spoon.

5. Bring the mixture together with your hands and form into small balls that will later fit into petit four cases. As you make the balls, place each one on the baking tray. Then place the tray in the fridge so the balls firm up.

6. After about an hour, melt the dark chocolate in the microwave or in a bowl over a pan of hot water.

7. Remove the cake balls from the fridge and use a cocktail stick to dip each one into the melted dark chocolate. As the balls should be chilled the chocolate should firm up quite quickly so they can be put straight into the petit four cases.

8. Chill for 20 minutes before placing in airtight containers. They will keep for about 7 days.

Variations
- Add 30g chopped glacé or dried cherries and substitute the rum for kirsch.

- For children's parties, simply replace the rum with 3 tablespoons chocolate syrup or orange juice for a fruitier version.

HOT CHOCOLATE STIRRERS

These are a wonderfully quick and fun gift idea to go along with a mug and a packet of good quality drinking chocolate. They are easy to make and are great to do with the children, who can be in charge of decoration. A good idea is to make a batch of white, milk and dark chocolate stirrers, and package them together with a lovely big bow.

MAKES 10–15

100g good quality chocolate
Decorations of your choice (e.g. chocolate chips, mini marsh-mallows, Smarties, chocolate buttons, chopped toffee)
Pack of decorative plastic spoons
(or metal ones, if you're pushing the boat out!)

---

1. Gently melt the chocolate in a bowl over a simmering pan.

2. Lay your spoons on a flat surface, concave side up. Carefully pour a tablespoon of melted chocolate into the well of each spoon.

3. Whilst the chocolate is still liquid, decorate each spoon with the treat of your choice. Leave to cool.

4. To present these, simply place them chocolate-side down into a cellophane greetings card bag. Gather the cellophane closed at the neck of the spoons and secure in place with a brightly coloured ribbon or elastic band.

5. Store in a lidded container in a cool dark place. Keeps for 2 weeks.

Variation

Another more luxurious way of making these is to use a large ice cube tray. Fill each section with one-third milk, one-third white and one-third dark chocolate (leaving each layer to set in between). As you make the last layer, force a long teaspoon into the melted chocolate and hold in place until sturdy. Leave to cool, then remove from the tray and present individually wrapped in small cellophane bags. Again, these will keep for 2 weeks in a lidded container.

Chapter Four
Sugaring and Candying Fruit and Nuts

A combination of candied fruit and nuts makes an excellent gift at Christmas time. Though some of the processes are rather long winded, it is worth doing at least once because it gives you a great sense of pride and satisfaction when you present the end result.

Sugared almonds are a perennial wedding favour. By simply wrapping them in a little bit of net fabric (to match the bridesmaid's dresses, of course) and a contrasting ribbon you have some quick presents for your guests, which are especially impressive if you have made them yourself!

Sugaring and candying fruit and nuts is a great way of preserving your own produce, especially to stock up your cupboard for baking, so any excess home grown fruit or nuts can be used for a few weeks extra.

SUGARED ALMONDS: THE MICROWAVE METHOD

I use the microwave to make Sugared Almonds as it is easier and less messy. You can use hazelnuts if you prefer or make a combination of both. For a festive flavour, add 1 teaspoon ground cinnamon to the sugar before microwaving for the first time.

MAKES 200G

---

6 rounded tablespoons golden caster sugar
Pinch salt
2 tablespoons water
200g whole almonds, skins left on

---

1. Cover a baking sheet with silicone paper.

2. Put the sugar, salt and water in a microwavable bowl and give it a quick stir. Place in the microwave and cook on high for 1 minute. Then stir.

3. Stir in the almonds and cook on high for 90 seconds.

4. Remove and stir and repeat this once more.

5. Transfer the hot mixture to the baking sheet and separate any nuts stuck together with a fork. Allow the nuts to cool completely.

6. Store in an airtight container. They will keep fresh for about 3 weeks.

Sugared Almonds: The Pan Method

MAKES 200G

100ml water
150g soft brown or golden caster sugar
Pinch salt
200g whole almonds, skins left on

---

1. Cover a baking sheet with silicone paper.

2. Put the water, sugar and salt into a deep frying pan over a low heat. Stir until all the sugar has dissolved.

3. Bring the syrup to the boil and boil for 1 minute.

4. Stir in the almonds and coat well in the mixture. Keep boiling all together for about 4 minutes or until the syrup has caramelised and thickened.

5. Transfer the sugared almonds to the baking sheet and use a fork to separate them. Allow the nuts to cool completely.

6. Store in an airtight container. They will keep fresh for about 3 weeks.

Variations
- Add 1 teaspoon vanilla or almond extract to the mixture as you add the nuts to the syrup.
- Add 1 teaspoon ground cinnamon at the same time as the nuts.

Candying Fruit

This is quite a lengthy process and takes days to complete, though only a few minutes of your time each day. It is a great way to preserve fruit you have grown yourself and they can be kept in an airtight container for use in cooking if you are not giving them as gifts.

It is a matter of replacing the water content of the fruit with sugar. This preserves the fruit for many months, so can be done well in advance of Christmas for example.

You must use perfect fruit and remember to blanch it in boiling water before soaking it in the syrup. This process softens the fruit so it will absorb the syrup.

Preparing and Blanching

Cherries - pit them if you wish and blanch for 15 seconds.

Citrus fruit – slice into thin segments and blanch for 15 seconds.

Apricots and plums – cut in half, de-stone and blanch for 20 seconds.

Apples and pears – cut into thick slices and blanch for 20 seconds.

Peaches – peel and cut into slices, and blanch for 10 seconds.

Quantities

For every 500g fruit use 250g caster sugar and 300ml water. Start with a small amount of fruit until you get used to the process, then use more as you feel more confident. More caster sugar is required each day so have the bag ready to weigh out each amount.

How to Candy Fruit

For best results it will take 6 days to make the finished candied fruit. This is a laborious process, but well worth it, especially if you are using excess fruit you have grown yourself.

Day One

- Prepare the fruit and make the first syrup. Put 250g caster sugar in a pan with 300ml water. Stir over a low heat until the sugar has fully dissolved.
- Bring to the boil then turn down the heat and simmer for 2–3 minutes.
- Lower the fruit carefully into the pan with a long-handled spoon. Remember that the sugar remains extremely hot!
- Stir the fruit gently so that it is all covered in the syrup. Cover when cool and leave in the pan for 24 hours.

Day Two

- Carefully lift the fruit from the syrup and place in a bowl. Some of the syrup will adhere to the fruit – you don't have to remove it all. Set aside.
- Add another 75g caster sugar to the syrup in the pan and stir over a low heat until this additional sugar dissolves. Bring to the boil and continue to boil for 1 minute. Then remove from the heat.
- Place the fruit back into this hot syrup, cover when cool and leave for 24 hours.

Day Three, Four, Five

- Repeat Day 2 but add 50g sugar.

Day Six

- Nearly there now! Drain the fruit as before but add 150g caster sugar to the syrup. Dissolve the sugar in the syrup over a low heat.
- Bring to the boil and boil for 1 minute. Then turn the heat down

to a simmer and add the fruit. Simmer everything together for 3 minutes, then leave to cool. When cool, cover and leave for 48 hours.

- Finally drain the fruit of as much syrup as you can. Some will adhere – this is no problem. Then place on a fine meshed cooling rack and leave in the air to dry out, which will take about 7 hours.

- Store in an airtight tin, away from heat and any damp. They will easily get soggy if they come into contact with any moisture. Alternatively, keep the fruits in the syrup until you are ready to give them away as gifts.

Presentation
- You can present the fruits in the syrup in decorative jars.
- I like to present a gift of sugared nuts and candied fruits together. I buy a container with two compartments and place the nuts in one and the fruits in another. Due to their sticky coating, use a layer of silicone paper to line the container.

Toffee Apples

These are good for all the year round, not just Bonfire Night. You can coat your apples with caramel, chocolate and a light sticky toffee that hardens and goes crispy.

Use ripe apples with no blemishes. Very crisp ones like Granny Smith's have quite tough skins, making them difficult to eat. Try Cox's, Braeburn or Royal Gala apples. If you have some growing in your garden, use those.

HOW TO MAKE TOFFEE APPLES

The familiar crispy toffee apples that are a favourite on Bonfire Night. Be careful when dipping into hot toffee – wear gloves to prevent injury!

Makes 6

---

6 apples
220g soft brown sugar
100ml water
½ teaspoon white vinegar
2 tablespoons golden syrup
25g butter

---

1. Line a baking sheet with silicone paper.

2. Wash the apples well and remove the stalks. Push a wooden lolly stick through the ends where the stalks have been.

3. Place the sugar and water in a pan over a low heat and stir until all the sugar has dissolved.

4. Stir in the vinegar, syrup and butter. Allow the butter to melt and combine with the other ingredients. Bring to the boil.

5. Using a thermometer, bring the temperature to 138°C (280°F), soft crack stage. Remove from the heat and immediately dip the apples into the toffee. Swirl them around to coat evenly and place on the baking sheet. Allow to cool fully before eating – don't be tempted to try them before then as you will burn your mouth!

6. Store in a cool, dark place. They will keep for 5–7 days.

Chocolate Apples

This is a much easier process than creating toffee apples. Simply use the techniques for Enrobing Fruit with Chocolate (page 37), though you will need to use a lolly stick rather than a cocktail stick to dip the apple into the chocolate.

You may find it easier (unless you wish to melt a large quantity of chocolate) simply to spoon your chocolate onto the apple to ensure it is fully (and generously) coated, as a shallow bowl of chocolate may not cover well. I find a mixture of dipping and spooning the chocolate onto the fruit works really well.

It is nice to roll your coated apple in chopped nuts, hundreds and thousands or chocolate drops whilst the chocolate is still warm. Try using a contrasting colour, so white chocolate drops on milk chocolate and vice versa.

You can buy pre-coloured chocolate buttons for melting if you wish to use different colours. They are available from larger craft shops (specifically those which have a cake decoration section) and online.

Chapter Five

Making Traditional Sweets

Sweet shops are wonderfully tempting places and, thankfully, seem to be having a resurgence on the local high street. We have three within ten minutes (by car), all of which have the shelves of jars containing our traditional favourites, as well as the more modern ones. Some of them are truly factory only, especially those that use coloured sugars twisted into unusual shapes, or soft centres, but others, specifically those sweets that have been made for decades as treats for all the family, are suprisingly easy to make at home. Everyone has their favourite, some are much easier to make than you would imagine and are doubly impressive as gifts. You may not need to go to the sweet shop again, though it's still a lovely thing to have a browse and get some ideas...

ACID DROPS

These are very easy to make. By adding a few drops of food colouring to the mixture, you can make them any colour – traditionally they are pale yellow, but it is up to you. Use a preserving thermometer for this recipe as it makes it easier to see when the mixture reaches a hard crack.

Makes about 300g

60ml water
200g sugar
120ml golden syrup
½ level teaspoon cream of tartar
1 level teaspoon
citric acid

---

1. Line two level baking trays with baking paper.

2. Put all the ingredients except for the citric acid in a sturdy pan and stir over a low heat until the sugar dissolves.

3. Raise the heat. When the mixture begins to boil, use a preserving thermometer to gauge when it reaches 150°C (302°F) or a hard crack.

4. Remove the pan from the heat and stir in the citric acid. The mixture will bubble at first, then settle.

5. When the mixture stops bubbling, grease a teaspoon and drop small amounts of the mixture onto the lined baking trays. Leave a little space between each drop to allow for spreading.

6. Allow to cool completely before dusting very lightly with icing sugar.

7. Remove carefully from the tray and wrap in pieces of cellophane. These will keep for 4 weeks in an airtight tin.

Useful Tip
Acid drops may go sticky if left out in the air, so always keep them in a good, airtight container.

BARLEY SUGAR DROPS

*Traditionally, barley sugars were made with barley extract and the
mixture was twisted into sugar canes as gifts at Christmas. They are
a delicious favourite that make brilliant coloured sweets by adding a
drop or two of food colouring to the mixture at the beginning.*

MAKES ABOUT 450G

150ml water
450g golden caster sugar
Juice & zest of 1 lemon*
½ level teaspoon cream of tartar

---

* Always use an unwaxed lemon for best results

1. Line two baking trays with baking paper.

2. Put all the ingredients together in a sturdy pan over a low heat
   and stir until the sugar has completely dissolved.

3. Raise the heat and bring to the boil. Measure the temperature
   with a preserving thermometer and when it reaches 150°C
   (302°F) or a hard crack remove from the heat.

4. Grease a teaspoon and drop small amounts of the mixture onto
   the prepared baking trays.

5. Leave to cool completely before wrapping in pieces of
   cellophane. Keeps for 4–6 weeks in an airtight tin.

BUTTERSCOTCH

This is a creamy, vanilla-flavoured Scottish sweet, and quite similar to sweets popular with grandparents the world over. I must admit, there is always a stash of butterscotch in my glove box to tide me over on long car journeys. You will usually find these wrapped in gold foil in the pick and mix counter, though be careful, if they are not stored in an airtight container they can go sticky, making them something of a chore to unwrap. A Kilner jar or a small tin will do the job perfectly.

MAKES ABOUT 500G

150ml water
1 teaspoon lemon juice
500g golden caster sugar
½ level teaspoon cream of tartar
100g unsalted butter
½ teaspoon vanilla extract

1. Grease and line a square, shallow baking tin with baking paper.

2. Put the water, lemon juice, sugar and cream of tartar in a pan over a low heat and stir until the sugar has completely dissolved.

3. Raise the heat and bring to the boil. Once the mixture is boiling, remove it from the heat and beat in the butter and vanilla.

4. Return to the heat and allow to boil, measuring the temperature with a thermometer. When it reaches the soft crack stage, 140°C (284°F), pour into the prepared tin.

5. Allow to cool for about 5 minutes, then score into squares with a knife and leave to cool completely.

6. When cold, break into pieces. It won't break into equally formed pieces and how it breaks will depend on how deep the mixture was scored. Wrap in cellophane or waxed paper. Keeps for 4–6 weeks in an airtight tin.

Coconut Ice

Traditionally, coconut ice is coloured white and pink, but you can make it any colour you wish. Why not add a few drops of peppermint extract and colour half the batch green and a few drops of lemon oil to colour the other half yellow. Half black and half orange makes a great Halloween treat, as does red and green for Christmas presents. Just have fun!

It is easier to make the mixture in two batches. This enables you to mix the colour in at the beginning of the preparation of the second batch so that it mixes thoroughly. Traditional recipes use caster sugar, but I find it a bit gritty. Icing sugar gives a smoother result.

MAKES 28–32 PIECES

---

2 x 125g icing sugar
2 x 100g condensed milk
2 x 100g desiccated coconut
A few drops of pink or your choice of food colouring*

---

* always measure this onto a spoon – don't be tempted to add it straight to the mixture as I have done!

1. Line a small loaf tin with a piece of baking paper placed on the bottom and coming up two sides to the top of the tin. This enables you to lift the coconut ice out easily, without using a rolling pin.

2. Sieve 125g icing sugar into a mixing bowl. Add 100g condensed milk and 100g coconut and mix well with a spatula.

3. Dust your hands with a little icing sugar and knead everything together. Press into the base of the tin and smooth out evenly.

4. Mix the second quantity of ingredients together including the food colouring. Combine well with your hands and press down evenly on top of the white layer.

5. Have a cooling rack ready, as this is the best way of getting the air to dry out the surface of the ice. Carefully lift the block of ice out of the tin and place on the rack. Dust very lightly with icing sugar and smooth over the surface, doing the same on the underside.

6. Leave for 3 hours. Then cut into squares, not too small but about 2cm, and leave to dry for another 2–3 hours before placing in an airtight container.

7. Make sure the container is airtight, as if not the ice will continue to dry out and become inedible within days. Otherwise this will keep for about 4 weeks.

EDINBURGH ROCK

This is not at all like those sticks found by the beach with the placename running through the centre. In fact, it has a softish, crumbly texture and is thought to date back to the early 19th century. It is quite easy to make and is best turned into bite-sized pieces rather than rolled into sticks like its harder counterpart.

MAKES 28–32 PIECES

450g white caster sugar
150ml water
½ level teaspoon cream of tartar
A few drops of peppermint oil

---

1. Line one baking tray with baking paper and oil a second tray.

2. Put the sugar and water into a sturdy pan and heat gently, stirring continuously until the sugar dissolves.

3. Raise the heat and cook to almost boiling without stirring. When the bubbles appear, remove from the heat and stir in the cream of tartar.

4. Place back on the heat and bring to the boil. Use a thermometer to gauge when the mixture reaches 121°C (250°F), hard ball stage. Remove from the heat.

5. Stir in the peppermint oil. Leave for 3 minutes to cool slightly.

6. Pour the mixture onto the oiled baking tray. Wearing clean rubber gloves, use a spoon to push the mixture back into itself as it cools. Whilst it is still hot but you are able to handle it wearing gloves, pull and fold the mixture 4–5 times. Roll into a long thin sausage shape and cut into bite-sized pieces with scissors.

7. Place the pieces on the paper-covered baking tray to completely cool. Leave open to the air overnight before storing in an airtight container.

Everton Toffee

We tend to think of minty sweets having the name 'Everton', usually black and white striped (like their footballing counterpart's strip). In fact, this is a brittle, buttery flavoured toffee to which you can add a few drops of peppermint if you like a minty flavour. Traditionally this toffee is made simply using these four ingredients.

MAKES ABOUT 500G

450g granulated sugar
¼ teaspoon cream of tartar
150ml water
80g unsalted butter, cut into small pieces

---

1. Line an 18cm square tin with silicone paper.

2. Place the sugar, cream of tartar and water in the pan. Heat gently, stirring over a low heat. When the sugar starts to dissolve, add the butter evenly over the surface of the sugar. Stir to combine.

3. When the butter has melted, stir once more then bring the mixture to the boil without stirring.

4. Bring the mixture to 152°C (305°F), hard crack stage. Allow it to cool slightly, then pour into the tin.

5. When almost set, score into the toffee with a sharp knife all the way through. This will help when breaking it into pieces.

6. Cool completely and break up into fairly evenly sized pieces. Wrap and store in an airtight container. Keeps for 4–6 weeks.

Useful Tip
To make this into Everton mints, add 3-4 drops of peppermint extract at the end of the cooking time to preserve the minty flavour.

FRUIT FONDANTS

These fondants can be dipped in chocolate if you wish for a little extra decadence. Liquid glucose can be readily purchased in supermarkets, you will most likely find it in the baking ingredients section. Shaped moulds are useful in this recipe and you can even make some coloured sugar mice with it!

MAKES ABOUT 450G

450g caster sugar
150ml warm water
25ml liquid glucose
Strawberry, lemon and orange natural flavouring
Red and yellow food colouring

---

1. Put the sugar and water in the pan and heat gently, stirring until the sugar dissolves completely.

2. Stir in the glucose and then bring the mixture to the boil.

3. When the temperature reaches 116°C (240°F), soft ball stage, remove from the heat and transfer to a heat-resistant bowl. Use a wooden spoon to stir the fondant until it becomes smooth and opaque. Divide the mixture into 3 basins and cover. Leave in a cool place for about 8 hours or overnight.

4. To flavour and colour the fondant, place each bowl of mixture in turn over a pan of simmering water and as the fondant melts add your chosen flavour and colour. Stir in gently and pour into the moulds, or allow to cool and then roll into small balls. If you are making mice, when the fondant is firm remove from the mould and use silver cake decorating balls for eyes.

5. If you wish to dip them into chocolate, melt your desired chocolate and use a cocktail stick to dip each fondant.

6. Store in a lidded container in a cool place. They should keep for 2 weeks.

HONEYCOMB

This is so easy to make and it is a great ingredient for ice cream, muffins and cake toppings. It can be dipped into chocolate or simply eaten plain.

You can pour it into a lined baking tin if you like, but I find it better to have a baking sheet covered with baking paper ready and simply pour it out. It sets quickly on the paper.

MAKES 2 GIFTS

120ml golden syrup
200g golden caster sugar
1 level teaspoon bicarbonate of soda

---

1. Place a sheet of baking paper on a flat baking tray.

2. Put the syrup in a sturdy pan. Stir in the sugar. Don't do any more stirring now until you whisk in the bicarbonate of soda.

3. Place the pan over a low heat until the sugar begins to melt, then turn up the heat to high and watch it come to a fast bubble. Allow it to change colour to a deep golden brown – this will take about 2½ minutes. Remove from the heat.

4. Quickly sprinkle the bicarbonate of soda over the mixture. Whisk it in and watch it fizz up. Pour onto the tray and allow it to cool.

5. Use a rolling pin to bash the honeycomb into small pieces. Store in an airtight container. Keeps for about 4 weeks.

KENDAL MINT CAKE

A favourite with fell walkers and mountain climbers the world over, this extra sweet treat was developed to give emergency energy rations. It is very easy to make and, once it has set, either dip in chocolate or drizzle melted chocolate over the top. Use real peppermint oil or essence for this recipe, as the flavour is much better.

MAKES ABOUT 500G

500g white or brown sugar (I use white caster or soft light brown sugar)
150ml whole milk
1–1½ teaspoons peppermint oil or essence, according to taste

---

1. Grease and line a shallow, approximately 15cm square baking tin.

2. Put the sugar and milk into a pan and stir over a low heat until the sugar has completely dissolved.

3. Bring to the boil and continue to boil until the mixture reaches 115°C (240°F), soft ball stage.

4. Remove from the heat and allow to cool for 2 minutes. Then beat the peppermint oil into the mixture using a wooden spoon. The mixture will be very thick at this stage so this will require a bit of elbow grease.

5. Transfer the mixture to the tin and use a hot palette knife to smooth out the surface.

6. Allow to cool. Whilst it is cooling, cut into bars of your desired size. Store in a lidded container in a dark place. Keeps for up to 8 weeks.

MARSHMALLOWS

This recipe can be tricky to make at first, but it helps to have all your ingredients and utensils ready. A silicone spatula is very useful when making marshmallows as the mixture doesn't stick to it in the same way as to a wooden spoon.

This makes a wonderful gift for hot chocolate fans, especially if presented in a large mug with a packet of good quality drinking chocolate. You could even make a few of the hot chocolate stirrers on page 53 for a complete set!

MAKES 2 GOOD-SIZED GIFTS AND A TREAT FOR YOURSELF!

250ml water
About 20g gelatine leaves or 25g powdered gelatine
420g white caster sugar
220ml golden syrup or liquid glucose*
Pinch salt
2 teaspoons vanilla extract
About 150g icing sugar to dust

---

* The glucose gives a whiter finish

1. Choose a shallow, approximately 30 x 22cm baking tin and line the base with silicone paper.

2. Place 130ml of the water in a food processor, with the whisk attachments in place. Add the gelatine to soften, leaving it for about 10 minutes whilst you prepare the syrup.

3. Put the sugar, syrup or liquid glucose, the rest of the water and salt in the pan. Stir over a low heat until the sugar dissolves.

4. Bring to the boil and then begin to measure the temperature with a thermometer. When it reaches 115°C (240°F), soft ball stage, remove from the heat.

5. Start the food processor on a low speed and after about 20 seconds begin pouring the sugar syrup gradually into the gelatine mixture still on a slow speed.

6. When all the syrup has been mixed in, turn up the processor to high and leave for about 10 minutes or until the mixture has fluffed up and looks very thick.

7. Add the vanilla and continue to whisk for a few seconds.

8. Thickly dust the lined tin with icing sugar and use a spatula to spread the marshmallow mixture into the tin. It will be very sticky and a bit messy but, don't worry, this is normal.

9. Thickly dust the top with icing sugar and leave uncovered to stand for about 24 hours.

10. The next day, dust a work surface with icing sugar. Using a hot dry knife, score around the edge of the marshmallow to loosen it and cut it into squares. Transfer the squares to the work surface. It may be easier to remove the mallow from the tin and cut it on the work surface with a hot dry knife. Have a go and see which method you prefer. Make sure each side is coated in icing sugar.

11. Leave to dry out for about 10 hours, then pack in an airtight container. Keeps for 2–3 weeks.

MARZIPAN FRUITS

The wonderful thing about marzipan is that it can be moulded into any shape, not just fruits. Try little mice, snowmen for Christmas or vegetables for gardening friends' birthdays. This recipe does contain raw egg - water can be used instead but the marzipan will dry out very quickly and become crumbly.

MAKES ABOUT 650G

350g ground almonds
200g icing sugar
150g caster sugar
2 teaspoons lemon juice
3–5 drops almond extract, depending on how strong a flavour you like
1 egg, beaten
Red, green, yellow and brown food colouring

---

1. Mix the almonds, icing and caster sugars together in a large mixing bowl.

2. Combine the lemon juice and almond extract and stir into the dry ingredients.

3. Add sufficient egg to make a stiff but pliable mixture.

4. Lightly dust a work surface with icing sugar and knead the marzipan until smooth.

5. Divide the mixture into four equal portions. Colour one portion red by adding a few drops of colouring at a time, then make one portion green and one yellow. Leave one natural to dilute the colour of the other portions or as a reserve.

6. Shape the fruits as necessary using the appropriately coloured marzipan. You can make orange by mixing small quantities of the red and yellow mixture. Make the brown stripes on bananas or the seeds on strawberries using a cocktail stick dipped in brown food colouring. Store in an airtight container for up to 5 days.

Useful Tip

For a more creative approach, use a new, clean paintbrush (you can buy these from craft stores, specifically for use with food) and paint on the colours. This will give you a little more flexibility in producing detail. To ensure your paintbrush is clean, plunge into freshly boiled water for 2–3 minutes.

MICROWAVE PEANUT BRITTLE

This is the quickest and easiest peanut brittle to make and is a great gift for a hamper, though make sure your recipients are not allergic to nuts!

MAKES ABOUT 550G

220g unsalted peanuts (you can use salted, but dust off some of the salt before cooking)
220g golden caster sugar
120ml golden syrup
15g butter (salted gives the best flavour)
1 teaspoon natural vanilla extract
1 teaspoon bicarbonate of soda (optional but gives a light, honeycomb finish)

---

1. Place a piece of baking paper on a baking tray.

2. Put the peanuts, sugar and golden syrup in a glass, microwavable bowl and stir together.

3. Cook in the microwave on high for 5–6 minutes, depending on the strength of your microwave. The peanuts will brown slightly as it cooks.

4. Remove from the microwave and stir in the butter and vanilla.

5. Cook in the microwave for 2 minutes more. Then stir in the bicarbonate of soda, if you are using it.

6. Pour onto the tray and allow to set. Then break into pieces with a rolling pin. Store in an airtight container. Keeps for 4 weeks.

Nougat

I love nougat, especially the nutty type. The great thing about it is you can add your favourite dried fruit and nuts or just leave it plain. However, it is tricky to make and there are a few stages that need to be managed carefully. Just take your time – it took us quite a few tries before getting it right.

MAKES AROUND 700G OR 3 LARGE BARS

450g caster sugar
230g powdered glucose
150ml water
2 large egg whites
100–150g nuts* or dried fruit

*Chop or halve nuts for best results

1. You will need a shallow, rectangular baking tin measuring about 15 x 25cm. You can line it with edible rice paper if you like, as on this occasion silicone paper does stick for some reason. If you don't use rice paper, butter the tin well.

2. Place the sugar, glucose and water in a pan over a low heat. Stir until all the sugar has dissolved.

3. Bring to the boil. Then simmer for 10 minutes, making sure you use a thermometer to gauge the temperature until it reaches 120°C (250°F), firm ball stage. Do not stir at this stage.

4. Meanwhile, during this 10 minutes, place the egg whites in a clean bowl and use a food processor to whisk to stiff peaks. Then continue to whisk on a low setting. It is best to use a food processor for this as you will need both hands free to add the syrup and you need to continue to whisk after adding the syrup.

5. When the sugar syrup reaches the correct temperature, pour about a quarter of it in a thin steady stream into the egg whites. Make sure it is still whisking steadily.

6. Return the rest of the syrup to the heat and bring to the boil again. This time the temperature needs to reach 149°C (300°F), hard crack stage. Keep the egg white mixture whisking gently.

7. When the syrup is ready, pour into the egg whites as they continue to whisk gently.

8. Keep whisking for about 20 minutes or until the nougat is thick and has reduced in volume. If the mixture gets up the sides of the bowl use a palette knife that has been dipped in boiling water to scrape it down into the bowl.

9. When the 20 minutes is up, gradually add the fruit and nuts or whatever you wish to add.

10. Turn off the whisk and use the palette knife to transfer the nougat to the prepared tin. Keep the knife hot by dipping in boiling water and smooth the nougat out evenly in the tin.

11. Store in a lidded container in a cool, dark place. It should keep for up to 4 weeks.

Useful Tip
Powdered glucose can be purchased in large chemist shops or brewing stores.

PEPPERMINT CREAMS

A delicious, after dinner treat, wonderful dipped in dark chocolate. I have made these with egg whites and evaporated milk, but I find this combination gives a better flavour and texture.

MAKES 25–30, DEPENDING ON YOUR CUTTER

280g icing sugar
100g condensed milk
½–¾ teaspoon natural peppermint oil, depending on how minty you like it

---

1. Sieve the icing sugar into a mixing bowl and mix in the condensed milk and peppermint oil.

2. Bring everything together with your hands and knead lightly until smooth.

3. Lightly dust a work surface with icing sugar and roll the mixture out until it is about 6mm deep or as thick as you like. Cut out the sweets using a small cutter of any shape, but I find circles are the easiest to deal with.

4. Place on a baking sheet covered with a layer of baking paper and leave to dry for about 1 hour before storing in an airtight container. They will keep for about 4 weeks.

Useful Tip
Drizzle or dip into melted dark chocolate for even more luxury. Use the techniques shown for enrobing fruit on page 37 for best results.

Welsh Toffee (Loshin Du)

This is the delicious, brittle black toffee, made famous by gift shops all over the Welsh valleys. It is a traditional recipe, this one known as Loshin Du in the South, or Taffi Triog in the North. Essentially it is a treacle toffee, though is much darker and harder so please, beware of your teeth!

MAKES 2–3 GIFTS

120g butter
450g granulated sugar
4 tablespoons black treacle
2 tablespoons white vinegar
2 tablespoons warm water

---

1. Line a rectangular baking tin, measuring about 28 x 18cm, with baking paper, greasing the tin first so the paper sticks and doesn't move about.

2. Melt the butter in a sturdy pan and stir in the sugar and treacle. Add the vinegar and water, and stir well until the sugar has dissolved.

3. Bring to boiling point, then boil steadily for 15 minutes, or until a little of the toffee snaps when it is put into a bowl of cold water. Pour the toffee into the prepared tin.

4. Leave to cool for 30 minutes then score into squares.

5. When cold, break up the squares and wrap in cellophane or baking paper. Store in an airtight container. Keeps for 4 weeks.

Chapter Six
Baked Treats

For all those difficult-to-buy-for friends and families, homemade hampers are a wonderful choice, and they can usually be a much cheaper option. Hampers to be given as gifts can be easily bulked out with some tasty baked treats, with the added bonus of tasty leftovers for yourself!

Planning Your Hamper

The trick to baking treats that make wonderful gifts is to think about a few key factors before you start. Hampers are a great option, but they do need a little planning to get the best results.

Bite sized

Think about how you are presenting your treats. Presenting muffins in a container in which there is only room for three or four does not make a hugely impressive gift. If you are posting your gift, make sure you find a container that will be sturdy enough and pack them so your recipient receives a yummy treat, rather than a mangled mess of crumbs.

Give Yourself Time

Making elaborate cakes with 5 minutes to spare is not only stressful, but really doesn't show off the thought that counted. Practise making your gift well in advance so you know you'll get it right. That way, you'll be able to eat the practice run too!

If In Doubt, Ice

If all you can run to is some simple shortbread, a bit of royal icing can make it look like the most impressive shortbread in the world. Getting to grips with a piping bag can take a bit of time, but if you want to start giving home-baked treats regularly, it's a valuable skill to master. Similarly, if you only have time for some white icing, hundreds and thousands will give it a party feel with very little effort. Turn to page 112 for advice and ideas on icing your gifts, and page 142 for tips on presenting them.

MINI MUFFINS

A great option for posting, you can present these scrumptious little efforts in a gift box meant for books and pop them in the letterbox. Truffle cases are widely available in many different colours and you can top them with whatever sweetie takes your fancy. Also, as they are so little, you can afford to make the mixture extra rich!

MAKES 1 GENEROUS GIFT

100g butter
100g golden caster sugar
1 egg
1 tablespoon golden syrup
100g self-raising flour

---

1. Preheat the oven to 150°C (Gas Mark 2–3). Place truffle cases in a muffin tray, two cases per muffin unit.

2. In a large bowl, cream together the butter and sugar until light and fluffy.

3. Add the egg, syrup and self-raising flour. Beat until fully incorporated.

4. Using a teaspoon, three-quarters fill each truffle case. Bake for 7–10 minutes. The cakes will be golden and should spring to the touch.

5. Store in an airtight container and they will keep for 5–7 days.

Icing

150g icing sugar
30ml water (you may not need to use it all)

1. Place the icing sugar in a bowl, add a teaspoon of water and then mix. Continue to add a teaspoon of water at a time, mixing until the icing is the consistency of gloss paint.

2. Spoon a little icing onto each cake and top with a sweetie of your choice. Good options are Dolly Mixtures, Smarties, Maltesers, Mini Eggs and Gummi Bears.

3. To make coloured icing, place a few drops of food colouring into the bowl with the icing sugar before you add the water. Then dilute as necessary.

AMARETTI BISCUITS

Coffee lovers unite! These little biscuits are frequently served with a nice espresso at the end of an Italian meal, and are a perfect gift for fans of amaretto and almond flavours. For an authentic way of presenting them, individually wrap each biscuit in thin waxed paper and place in a Kilner jar finished with a ribbon. Buon appetito!

MAKES 2 GIFTS

140g butter
3 egg whites
220g golden caster sugar
220g ground almonds
1 tablespoon amaretto liqueur (optional)

---

1. Preheat the oven to 150°C (Gas Mark 2–3) and line a baking tray with paper.

2. Soften the butter by creaming it in a large bowl.

3. Whisk the egg whites until they become foamy but do not allow them to form soft peaks.

4. Add the sugar and ground almonds to the butter and mix. Add the egg whites and amaretto liqueur and mix well. The mixture should be fairly stiff.

5. Using a teaspoon, place balls of the mixture, no bigger than 2½cm in diameter, onto the baking tray, leaving plenty of room between each one.

6. Bake for 20 minutes, until golden brown. Store in an airtight container and they will keep for 4–6 days.

7. For coconut lovers, replace the almonds with dessicated coconut, and the amaretto with coconut liqueur for a Caribbean flavour.

COOKIE LOLLIES

These cookies make a great option for a children's party or stocking fillers at Christmas. They can be presented by covering the cookie end with a cellophane bag (available from good craft shops, especially those that sell equipment for making greeting cards) and finishing with a ribbon. Adding brightly coloured chocolate beans gives them an extra party flavour. Also, if you make them in conjunction with a batch of amaretti biscuits, you'll be able to use up the egg yolks you saved from the recipe! You will need some lolly sticks to make these cookies, which are available from most craft stores.

MAKES 10–12

150g butter
150g golden caster sugar
Addition of your choice (see variations below)
3 egg yolks
300g plain flour

---

1. Cream together the butter and sugar. Add the addition of your choice.

2. Beat the egg yolks in a separate bowl and add them a little at a time, alternating with the flour, to the butter and sugar mix until fully incorporated. You should have a firm dough. If the dough looks too sticky, add a little more flour. Alternatively, you may not need to use all the egg.

3. Roll the mixture into a 5cm-thick cylinder and cover with cling film. Chill for 2 hours.

4. Preheat the oven to 180°C (Gas Mark 4) and line two baking trays with baking parchment.

5. Slice the cookie dough into 1½cm circles and place on the baking tray, saving a little of the dough to secure the sticks. Press a lolly stick into each circle, securing in place with a little more dough.

6. Bake for 18–20 minutes, until golden brown. Store in an airtight container and they will keep for 5–6 days.

Variations
You can add anything to this mixture, from chocolate pieces, nuts, raisins, fruit pieces, even sweeties. Be as creative as your (or your recipient's) tastebuds allow!

GINGER BISCUIT SHAPES

You can buy a range of cookie cutters from most craft shops, and even some larger supermarkets will offer a few more options for creative baking. Gingerbread is an easy staple that can be iced to look like something wonderfully expensive and personal.

If you can't find a suitable cutter, simply draw out your desired shape on a piece of thin plastic (an ice cream tub lid works brilliantly) and cut it out with a pair of solid scissors. Use this as a template to trace round with a sharp knife. This takes longer than using a cutter, but enables you to make gingerbread fish, letters, bows or whatever takes your fancy.

Iced gingerbread makes a wonderfully personal (not to mention delicious) wedding favour. You could cut out guests' initials, thus removing the need for place cards (every little expense spared adds up!), or simply ice their names on small biscuits. If you practise your piping beforehand, you'll be surprised how quickly you will pick this up. For more tips on icing, turn to page 112.

MAKING GINGER BISCUITS

MAKES 8–12

100g golden caster sugar
300g self-raising flour
1 teaspoon ground ginger
A little milk
150g butter, at room temperature

---

1. Preheat the oven to 175°C (Gas Mark 3-4) and grease a large baking tray with oil or butter.

2. Place the sugar, flour and ginger in a bowl and stir well.

3. Ensure the butter is at room temperature before cubing the block into small pieces. Add this to the dry ingredients.

3. Rub the fat into the flour. This will soon resemble breadcrumbs.

4. Using a little milk (be sparing, only a tablespoon may be needed), moisten the crumbs and bring together to form a dough that resembles sweet pastry.

5. Once you have all the dough in a single ball, dust a work surface with flour and roll out the dough to 1cm thick.

6. Cut out your shapes and carefully place them onto the baking tray. Bake for 12–15 minutes until golden brown and firm. (Keep an eye on them as they will soon catch and won't make good gifts if burnt!)

7. Cool on a wire rack and decorate as desired. Ensure the biscuits are fully cooled before decorating.

8. Store in an airtight container. They will keep for about 7 days.

Variations
- For vanilla biscuits, replace the ginger with 1 teaspoon vanilla extract.
- For chocolate biscuits, replace the ginger with 25g cocoa powder (you may need a little more milk to encourage this into a ball).
- For citrus biscuits, replace the ginger with a little lemon, lime or orange zest.

Edible Christmas Decorations

To make a ginger biscuit for the tree, use the recipe above and, after cutting out your shape (a star or bauble shape works well), use a clean drinking straw to cut a hole 1cm from the top. Bake as normal then thread a festive ribbon through the hole for hanging on the tree. These make a fantastic gift for Christmas visits, especially if presented in a big red box!

DIANA'S SIGNATURE SHORTBREAD

This is truly a family favourite, is so versatile and will become the go-to baking treat once tried. Below are some wonderful variations to the recipe to allow you to make a whole range of treats your friends and family will love.

MAKES ABOUT 12 PORTIONS

150g plain flour
50g self-raising flour
130g butter, softened
120g soft brown sugar or golden caster sugar

1. Preheat the oven to 180°C (Gas Mark 4) and grease either a 20cm round sandwich tin or an 18 x 28cm rectangular one.

2. Sift the two flours together in a mixing bowl.

3. Add the butter in small pieces and rub it into the flour with your fingertips until it resembles breadcrumbs.

4. Stir in the sugar and use your hands to bring the dough together. Massage the mixture gently until it forms a smooth, pliable dough.

5. Press into the prepared tin and bake for about 20–25 minutes or until golden brown.

6. Leave to cool for 5 minutes then cut into the desired sized pieces, but leave them in the tin to go cold. Store in an airtight container. Keeps for about a week.

Iced Shortbread
For a bit of extra sweetness, make up some glacé icing as show on page 113 and drizzle over the shortread before cutting them up at stage 6. Leave to set and then cut into pieces.

Chocolate Shortbread
A delicious chocolatey version can be made by replacing 30g cocoa at stage 2, sifting it in with the flour. Follow the recipe as above.

You can serve it as it is, or melt some chocolate (as shown on page 35) and drizzle on top, refrigerating until solid. This is guaranteed to become a firm favourite with chocolate fans.

Cherry Shortbread
A must for cherry lovers, simply add 60g chopped or halved glacé cherries or dried fruit of your choice to the dough at stage 4. For a boozy version, soak the fruit in a liqueur or brandy for 24 hours before beginning.

Millionaire's Shortbread
Truly a treat worth a million dollars. Top the basic shortbread recipe by spreading caramel mixture (see Soft Caramel, page 28) at stage 6, before cutting into the desired pieces. Refrigerate this for a few hours until the caramel sets slightly.

Melt 150g chocolate of your choice (by using the guide on page 35) and spread it over the caramel layer. Refrigerate for another 2 hours before cutting into generous pieces. You may need to dip your knife into hot water to stop the chocolate layer cracking.

GRANDMA'S STREUSEL TRAY BAKE

This streusel is delicious for a hamper, especially if you make the jam yourself and add a jar of it to the basket. It works really well cut into strips of around 5 x 10cm and is a delicious teatime treat.

MAKES 1 GIFT

Base
100g butter
50g caster sugar
100g plain flour
6 tablespoons jam

Topping
125g self-raising flour
100g butter
75g soft brown sugar
25g oats
Zest of 1 lemon

---

1. Preheat the oven to 175°C (Gas Mark 3–4). Lightly oil a 20 x 30cm tin.

2. Beat together the butter and caster sugar until pale. Slowly stir in the plain flour to form a soft dough.

3. Press the dough into the tin and bake for 15 minutes.

4. Once out of the oven, spread the entire surface with the jam.

5. To make the topping, add the flour to a bowl and rub in the butter until it resembles breadcrumbs.

6. Stir in the sugar, oats and lemon zest. This should look like a crumble topping mixture.

7. Spread the topping over the jam and bake again for 35–40 minutes until golden.

8. Allow to cool before cutting into slices. Store in an airtight container. Keeps for 5–6 days.

Variation

For a decadent chocolate version, use chocolate spread instead of jam. Add 25g cocoa powder to both the base and topping recipes and drizzle dark chocolate over the top after the bake has cooled.

CELEBRATION FLAPJACKS

These favourite flapjacks can be made even better by modifying the recipe slightly for any occasion. First, get the hang of the basic recipe, which is great, and then choose from the variations to make it sensational. Present the flapjacks in bite-sized pieces, displayed in an extra large Kilner jar. The jar won't stay full for long!

MAKES 10–12 PORTIONS

150g butter
150g golden caster sugar
2 tablespoons golden syrup
330g porridge oats

---

1. Preheat the oven to 180°C (Gas Mark 4) and grease an 18 x 28cm rectangular baking tin.

2. Put the butter, sugar and syrup in a pan over a low heat and allow the butter to melt into the other ingredients. Stir to combine.

3. Stir in the oats and make sure they are well coated in the butter mixture.

4. Press the mixture down into the prepared baking tin. I find using the back of a metal spoon is the easiest for this.

5. Bake for 20–25 minutes.

6. Cut into slices whilst it is still hot and then leave in the tin to cool. This should keep fresh in an airtight tin for 7–8 days.

See the next page for some delicious variations...

Triple Chocolate Flapjacks

1. Add 100g melted chocolate to the pan before the oats, then 25g cocoa after.

2. Mix thoroughly and bake as usual.

3. Once cooled, cut into chunks or slices and drizzle with white chocolate.

Apple and Cinnamon Flapjacks

1. Add 2 teaspoons cinnamon to the wet ingredients and 50g diced dried apple when adding the oats.

2. Stir thoroughly and bake as usual.

3. For an extra kick, add 25ml Calvados to the pan before adding the oats.

Bonfire Flapjacks

1. Replace half the syrup with black treacle.

2. Bake as usual.

3. For an extra snap, crackle and pop, sprinkle the flapjack with popping candy and top with chocolate.

LEMON DRIZZLE CAKES

Perfect for a summer's gift, a basket of lemon drizzle cakes are a lovely accompaniment to a chilled glass of homemade lemonade. If you can find them, use yellow cupcake cases and top each cupcake with a bit of candied lemon peel.

MAKES 15

150g butter
150g caster sugar
2 eggs
150g self-raising flour
Juice of 1 lemon
Zest of 1 lemon

Topping
Juice of 3 lemons
50g golden granulated sugar

---

1. Preheat the oven to 175°C (Gas Mark 3–4) and add the cake cases to a muffin tray.

2. Cream together the butter and sugar until pale and fluffy.

3. Add the eggs and flour, little by little, and beat until fully incorporated.

4. Add the lemon juice and zest and beat again.

5. Divide the mixture between the cake cases and bake for 20–25 minutes, or until risen, pale golden brown and they spring back when pressed lightly.

6. For the topping, combine the lemon juice and golden granulated sugar in a bowl. Prick each cake with a skewer a few times and pour 2 tablespoons of the mixture into each one.

7. Store in an airtight container. They will keep for 5–7 days.

Variation
To turn these into cupcakes, place a little less mixture in each cake case (so there is a space of around 1cm at the top of each case) and ice using recipe on page 113.

FLORENTINES

These delicious, nutty, fruity, chocolatey biscuits are a real treat and they are much easier to make than you would think. Make them just before you wish to give them as a gift – as the caramel gets sticky, they are at their best only for about four days.

MAKES ABOUT 12

50g plain flour
30g glacé cherries, chopped or sliced
30g raisins
30g pecans or walnuts, chopped
30g flaked almonds
80g butter
50g soft brown sugar
200g chocolate, around 60% cocoa solids is the best

---

1. Preheat the oven to 180°C (Gas Mark 4) and grease and line two baking sheets with silicone baking paper. Have two ready as it can get a bit messy trying to squeeze them onto one sheet.

2. Sift the flour into a mixing bowl and stir in the fruit and nuts.

3. Put the butter and sugar in a small pan and melt over a low heat. Stir until the sugar has dissolved.

4. Pour the butter mixture into the dry ingredients and combine gently with a wooden spoon.

5. Drop dessertspoons of the mixture onto the prepared baking sheets and press down lightly with the back of a metal spoon.

6. Bake for about 8–10 minutes.

7. Leave to cool on the baking sheet. When cool, use a palette knife or flat spatula to place them on a wire rack to go completely cold.

8. Meanwhile, melt the chocolate in a bowl over a pan of hot water. Thickly spread over the Florentines and allow to set before storing in an airtight tin. They will keep for 5–7 days.

CHOCOLATE TIFFIN

*A no-bake slice that is far too delicious for words or your waistline.
You can add as much or as little as you like, and tailor the recipe to
suit you. If your recipient is a fan of nuts, go to town with pecans,
brazil nuts and so on. If fruit is their fancy, raid the dried fruit
section of the supermarket.*

MAKES 16 BITE-SIZED OR 8 LARGER PIECES

200g dark chocolate
100g milk chocolate
3 tablespoons honey or golden syrup
120g butter
100g raisins
50g glacé cherries, halved
12 digestive biscuits

---

1. Butter an 18 x 18cm square tin.

2. Break up the chocolate into a pan and add the honey or syrup
   and butter. Place over a very low heat. Alternatively, put the
   mixture into a bowl over a simmering pan of hot water, on a
   low heat. Allow the ingredients to combine.

3. Crush the biscuits into small pieces (not going as far as
   crumbs). Put the fruit and crushed biscuits in a bowl and pour
   in the warm chocolate mixture. Stir everything together well
   and press down into the prepared tin.

4. Allow to cool, then place in the fridge for a couple of hours.

5. Cut into pieces. It will keep for 8–10 days.

CHOCOLATE BROWNIES

Quick and easy brownies are a treat anytime. They should be made just before they are given as a gift, as they lose their texture after about five days.

MAKES 1 GIFT

180g self-raising flour
20g cocoa powder
100g butter
180g soft brown or golden caster sugar
1 egg, beaten
50g real dark chocolate chips or dark chocolate broken into small pieces

---

1. Preheat the oven to 180°C (Gas Mark 4) and butter and line a 20cm square tin.

2. Sift the flour and cocoa powder into a mixing bowl.

3. Melt the butter and sugar together in a saucepan over a low heat. Pour into the flour and mix well with a wooden spoon.

4. Stir in the egg and chocolate to form a moist, soft dough.

5. Pour the mixture into the prepared tin and bake for 15–20 minutes or until the brownies are slightly springy to the touch but the surface is flat and firm.

6. Leave to cool in the tin for 20 minutes, then cut into slices of your desired size.

7. Transfer to a cooling rack and allow to cool completely before putting in an airtight tin. They will keep for about 5 days.

Variations
• Add 50g chopped walnuts or pecans with the chocolate chips.
• Soak 50g black or Morello cherries (I use defrosted frozen cherries) in a little kirsch for a few hours and stir into the mixture just after the chocolate at stage 4.

BASIC WHOOPIE PIES

The all-American classic has been well loved for decades across the pond and is a brilliant addition to any hamper as they can be adapted to be beautifully colourful. Whoopie pies resemble macaroons, but are more like a cross between a brownie and a cake when eaten. This basic mixture can be adapted in hundreds of ways to suit all tastes. For now, let's start at the beginning…

MAKES 2 GIFTS

---

1 egg
150g caster sugar
100g butter, melted
50ml double cream
200g self-raising flour
Milk to loosen

---

1. Preheat the oven to 180°C (Gas Mark 4).

2. Whisk the egg until light and fluffy.

3. Add the sugar and whisk again until fully incorporated.

4. Add the melted butter and cream.

5. Sift in the flour and stir in fully. If the batter appears a little too stiff, add some milk to loosen. The mixture should form soft peaks and be firm enough not to spread too much when spooned onto the baking tray.

6. Use an ice cream scoop to dollop mixture into 3½cm balls onto a greased baking tray, leaving about 3cm between the pies.

7. Bake for 13–15 mins, or until risen and firm. Leave to cool.

8. Store in an airtight container in a cool place. Keeps for 5–6 days.

Basic Icing

100g butter
200g icing sugar

---

1. Cream the butter until soft and fluffy, then sift in the icing sugar and beat. If the mixture is too loose, add more icing sugar.

2. Sandwich cooled pies together with the icing.

VARIATIONS ON A WHOOPIE THEME

Once you have made the basic Whoopie batter, it is very simple to adapt the recipe to alter the colour and flavour of the pies. To change the colour, simply divide your mixture into three bowls and add a couple of drops of different natural food colouring into each bowl. Then bake as described on page 109.

Chocolate Whoopies

40g cocoa powder
Splash of milk

---

1. Simply add the cocoa powder to the basic Whoopie batter and follow the recipe as shown on page 108. You may need a little splash of milk to loosen the mixture, then bake as normal.

2. Alternatively, add chocolate drops instead of or as well as (why not?) cocoa. Sandwich together using the chocolate icing mix shown below.

Chocolate Flavoured Icing

80g butter, melted
1 tablespoon golden syrup
30g cocoa
200g icing sugar

---

1. In a large bowl, stir the syrup into the melted butter.

2. Sift in the cocoa and stir into the mixture until it is fully incorporated. Then sift in the icing sugar and beat into the mixure.

3. Leave to cool before using to sandwich the pies. It is best to use a palette knife to get a smooth, even layer.

Cappuccino Icing
To turn your basic chocolate Whoopies into mocha flavour, why not try this delicious cappuccino icing...

40g butter, melted
1 teaspoon instant coffee, dissolved in 40ml warm milk
200g icing sugar

---

1. Melt the butter in a medium sized bowl and dissolve the coffee in the milk. Pour the coffee/milk mixture into the melted butter and stir.

2. Sift in the icing sugar and beat.

3. Leave to cool slightly before using to sandwich the pies.

Peppermint Cream Icing
A mint choc-chip treat works brilliantly with Chocolate Whoopies. Try sandwiching them with this delicious peppermint cream...

---

1 egg white
3 drops peppermint extract
2 drops green food colouring
250g icing sugar

---

1. Whisk the egg white until light and fluffy, then add the peppermint extract and food colouring.

2. Sift in the icing sugar and beat. Use the icing to sandwich the pies.

Chapter Seven
Decorating Your Sweets and Treats

There is something wonderfully magical about visiting a choco-laterie or patisserie, where the basic recipes are made to look a million dollars by a little clever decoration. A piece of fudge can be made into a masterpiece (and therefore a fantastically impressive present) by chopping it into a neat cube and piping a quick design onto it. Knowing how to make different types of icing enables you to make even the simplest recipe into a wonderfully personal and decorative gift. There are many types, all with varying degrees of difficulty, to suit all types of job. It does take a little time, but once the basic techniques are mastered, you can be confident in producing brilliant results for every occasion.

GLACÉ ICING

The simplest of icing is made from water and icing sugar. It can be used throughout baking for easy, delicious results (try it drizzled over Diana's Signature Shortbread (page 97) – it is wonderful!) and dries to a firm, soft icing in a couple of hours.

Glace icing is not really suitable for piping, so is best spooned carefully onto cakes or biscuits. However, it is quick to do and can be made with the children as you don't need any egg (so is a bit safer for small tums).

To gauge how much icing sugar you will need, use the rule of 20g of icing sugar to every inch (2½cm) in diameter of cake. So to ice 12 buns that are around 1½ inches (roughly 4cm) in diameter each, you'll need 360g icing sugar, depending on how generous you are feeling. If in doubt, add another inch, just to be sure.

1. Sift the icing sugar into a bowl and add water, a dessert-spoonful at a time. Stir until you have a thick, spreadable paste that coats the spoon and doesn't fall off.

2. If you wish to make coloured glacé icing, add 5 or 6 drops of food colouring before adding the water. Stir well. To make your icing deeper in colour, add more food colouring before adding the water.

3. If the icing becomes too thin, simply add a little more icing sugar until you reach your desired consistency.

FUDGE ICING

A delicious icing that works so well with chocolate cake. It is best slapped on thickly with a knife, and a dusting of cocoa or a little more icing sugar will make it look absolutely irresistible.

MAKES ENOUGH TO GENEROUSLY TOP A 20CM CAKE

50g butter, melted
40ml milk or cream
2-3 drops vanilla extract
250g icing sugar

---

1. Slowly melt the butter in a pan. Add the milk or cream and vanilla. Warm this through for 2–3 minutes but do not boil.

2. Sift the icing sugar into a large bowl and pour the wet ingredients over, beating quickly with a wooden spoon. The mixture should be thick and spreadable.

Variations
- For Chocolate Fudge Icing, add 70g melted dark chocolate to the wet ingredients before beating into the sugar.
- For Coffee Fudge Icing, add 1 teaspoon instant coffee granules (1 heaped teaspoon if you want a stronger flavour) to the warm milk before adding to the butter mixture. Alternatively, simply use a single espresso and 1 tablespoon cream instead of the milk.

ROYAL ICING

A favourite with all cake decorators, royal icing provides a wonderful, pliable icing that sets hard and holds its shape. You can make it in varying degrees of viscosity, from the fluid 'flood' style icing used on cupcakes and biscuits, to the slightly firmer piping variety, to the thick fondant icing used for covering celebration cakes.

Royal icing is a fantastic way of creating personal designs on your sweets, and works especially well with chocolate slabs or Easter eggs. Try practising your handwriting with a piping bag on some baking parchment before you begin to ensure you are confident.

The icing is made using icing sugar and egg white. Egg yolk should never be used, and the eggs should be as fresh as possible, as the icing is not cooked. Ideally, buy the eggs especially for the job and save the yolks for a custard or ice cream.

MAKING ROYAL ICING

---

1 egg white icing sugar

Recipe A
For flood icing, use 1 egg white per 130g icing sugar

Recipe B
For piping work and detail, use 1 egg white per 180g icing sugar

Recipe C
For icing cakes, use 1 egg white per 250g icing sugar

If you wish to use food colouring, be aware that you will need to use a little more icing sugar to reach the correct consistency.

1. Separate the egg white from the yolk and put the white in a large mixing bowl. Whisk it through with a fork to loosen.

2. Sift the necessary amount of icing sugar for your chosen icing into the bowl. If you are changing the colour of the icing, add 5–6 drops now and beat well. For best results, beat for as long as possible, by hand for around 15 minutes or 5 minutes with a slow electric mixer. If the colour is not vibrant enough, add a few more drops. If your icing starts to go too thin, sift in another 20g icing sugar.

Creating Designs with Royal Icing

If you have never used this type of icing before, it is best to buy an extra packet of icing sugar and eggs for trial runs. Once you get the hang of it, you'll never look back. For creating designs on cookies, follow these steps.

USE RECIPE B
1 egg white per 180g icing sugar

---

1. Use a slightly thicker consistency to create your basic outline first. Mix a colour for the outline using Recipe B on page 116 and the food colouring of your choice, then fill a piping bag fitted with a narrow nozzle. Force the icing right down to the tip and twist the end closed as shown below. Push a little icing out to get rid of any air holes and try and draw out the basic shape. To practise, simply draw out your shape on a piece of A4 paper and attempt to follow the line with your piping bag. Another practice tip is to try signing your name with icing on a piece of baking parchment.

2. The outline will act as a barrier, beyond which your flood icing will not spread. So make sure all areas you wish to fill in are completely enclosed by the outline, as any gaps will be breached.

3. Outline all the designs you wish to make before moving on to the next colour.

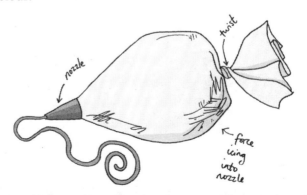

USE RECIPE A
1 egg white per 130g icing sugar

1. Make up your flood icing using Recipe A. If you need many different colours, separate the mixture into bowls or jam jars before adding your food colouring. Remember, the colouring will thin your mixture, so take this into account when mixing your basic icing.

2. Using a teaspoon (or dessertspoon for larger areas), simply spoon your icing into the space you have outlined. Add the other colours as necessary.

USE RECIPE B
1 egg white per 180g icing sugar

1. Leave the flood icing to dry for 10–15 minutes before piping any other details on top. Use Recipe B and the colour of your choice for this.

ICING CHOCOLATES AND FUDGE

USE RECIPE B
1 egg white per 180g icing sugar

Create an extra special look to your chocolates by using a piping bag filled with royal icing to pipe on delicate designs. Alternatively, simply melting white chocolate to drizzle on a milk chocolate will look delicious as well as beautiful. You can buy all sorts of coloured chocolates for decorating your sweets from many good craft and cake suppliers.

DECADENT MARSHMALLOWS

*Whether you've made marshmallows yourself or cheated and bought
a bag of them, you can create lovely sweet gifts using a little melted
chocolate and a packet of Smarties. This simple decoration also works
for other sweets, especially blocks of plain fudge.*

MAKES 1 GENEROUS GIFT OR PARTY PLATTER

---

30 marshmallows
50g milk chocolate
Packet of Smarties

---

1. Place the marshmallows on a plate or baking tray, leaving a gap
between each one.

2. Melt the chocolate in a bowl over a slowly simmering pan of
water. Then remove from the heat and leave to stand for 1
minute.

3. Using a teaspoon, spoon a little chocolate onto each
marshmallow and place a single Smartie on the top. Leave to
cool before placing in a shallow box and giving as a gift.

Chapter Eight

Making Preserves, Sweet Syrups & Alcoholic Beverages

Not everyone likes toffees and chocolates, but a homemade preserve, syrup or special drink makes a very welcome present. They can also be an integral part of putting together a homemade hamper, which is always a joy to receive. The gifts can be made extra special by investing in a glorious antique bottle, or using a pretty jar with a cloth topper, though the contents of these will be enough to make sure you are top of the Christmas card list every year!

The alcoholic drinks in this book don't require any fermenting, they simply use spirits blended with sweet syrups or chocolates to produce naughty, mouthwatering treats that are fantastic celebration items.

Preserves

I love making preserves, especially unusual ones. If you are making them to be given as Christmas presents, the fresh fruit is not always readily available. Bear in mind that you can also make excellent preserves using frozen fruit – your own from a summer glut or simply buy some from the shops. You can make as little as two 500g jars if you so wish or try making different flavours – it takes hardly any time or fuss.

The great thing about giving preserves is that they keep for much longer than toffees and chocolates, so you can make them in advance.

If you use jam sugar, which can be bought in supermarkets, you will find your jam sets beautifully and will take just minutes to boil.

Summer Fruit Jam

This jam is a combination of raspberries, blackcurrants, strawberries and redcurrants. It gives a taste of summer during the cold winter months. You can easily double the quantities if you wish.

MAKES ABOUT 2 X 500G JARS

500g frozen summer fruits
500g jam sugar
2 tablespoons crème de cassis (optional)

---

1. Sterilise the jam jars and their screwtop lids.

2. Place the fruit and sugar in a sturdy pan and stir to combine. Leave for 20 minutes.

3. Place the pan over a low heat and stir until the sugar has dissolved.

4. Bring to the boil and as soon as the mixture is boiling vigorously, start timing 4 minutes. Then remove from the heat.

5. Add the crème de cassis if using, stir well and leave for 5 minutes.

6. Ladle into the prepared jars and screw the lids on tightly.

7. When the jars are cold, label with the date and type of jam. Keeps for at least 12 months unopened.

Variation

• Some supermarkets sell packets of frozen black forest fruits which contain blackberries and black cherries. Try using them in this recipe instead of summer fruits. The end result is a very dark purple jam which makes an excellent filling or topping for chocolate cake.

Pina Colada Jam

This is easy if you use canned pineapple. You can make jam with fresh pineapple but make sure you weigh just the flesh and break it up into small pieces or use a processor to chop it finely.

MAKES ABOUT 2 X 500G JARS

560g tinned pineapple in its juice or fresh pineapple
100ml water or pineapple juice, if using fresh pineapple
500g jam sugar
Juice of 1 lemon
100g desiccated coconut
3 tablespoons rum

1. Sterilise the jam jars and their screwtop lids. As this recipe makes slightly more, also sterilise a small jar so you can treat yourself.

2. If you are using fresh pineapple, add 100ml water or pineapple juice along with the fruit to a pan. Simmer for 20 minutes until the fruit softens. If you are using tinned pineapple, simply place it a pan along with the juice from the tin.

3. Add the lemon juice. Stir in the sugar over a low heat until it has dissolved. Then add the coconut.

4. Bring to the boil and boil for 4 minutes. Remove from the heat and leave for 5 minutes.

5. Stir in the rum and ladle into the jars. Screw the lids on tightly. Label the jars when cold. Keeps for 6 months.

Variation
• Instead of rum, try adding 2 tablespoons pineapple liqueur.

PRUNE CONSERVE

This is a rich and very satisfying conserve that makes a great substitute for mincemeat in pies and tarts. It takes a little more preparation than the other recipes but is well worth the effort.

MAKES ABOUT 3 X 500G JARS

500g no-soak prunes
300g raisins
100g no-soak apricots, chopped
120g almonds, chopped or flaked
500ml water
5 tablespoons brandy
250g caster sugar
250g soft brown sugar
2 extra tablespoons brandy (optional)

---

1. Sterilise the jam jars and their screwtop lids.

2. Put the fruit and nuts in a bowl and pour over the water and brandy. Stir well so all the fruit is coated, cover with a clean tea towel and leave overnight to soak.

3. The next day put the fruit and nut mixture in a pan and stir in the caster and brown sugars over a low heat. Continue stirring the mixture until the sugar has dissolved.

4. Bring to the boil and boil for 5 minutes, stirring continuously.

5. Turn the heat down and simmer for 15–20 minutes or until the mixture has thickened.

6. Allow the mixture to cool a little and then stir in the extra brandy if using.

7. Ladle into the jars and screw the lids on tightly. Label the jars when cold.

Variations
- Use rum or whisky instead of brandy.
- Instead of 300g raisins, use 150g raisins, 50g chopped glacé cherries and 100g sultanas.
- Use chopped mixed nuts, pecans or walnuts instead of almonds.

Sweet Syrups

These syrups are ideal for serving with ice creams and desserts or diluted as a drink.

They do require a bit of preparation and scrupulously clean bottles and lids to prolong their life. Though corked bottles look quaint and traditional, they are not as practical as a screwcap bottle, which keeps the syrup in better condition for longer.

The quantity yield for making syrups of course depends on the amount of juice extracted from a batch of fruit. This is very difficult to measure until the fruit has been cooked, so always sterilise more than enough bottles for the batch of fruit you are preparing. As a very rough guide, 1kg of fruit gives between 200 and 400ml of juice depending on the type and ripeness.

The freshest tasting syrup is one that is heated for the least time. But if you want to store the syrup, boil the bottles after you have filled them. Place the sealed bottles in a pan and fill the pan with hot water until it reaches the neck. Use a preserving thermometer to measure 78°C (170°F) and maintain this temperature for 30 minutes. Remove the bottles from the pan very carefully using a pair of tongs or oven gloves. They will store for around 6 months.

BLACKCURRANT SYRUP

This is my favourite and the fruit usually gives a good juice yield. It is particularly good as an ice cream sauce and also added to gin or white wine as a summer drink.

Some recipes require you to boil the syrup but this spoils the fresh flavour of the fruit, so this recipe only heats the juice and sugar together. It has a far shorter shelf life but the taste is exquisite.

MAKES ABOUT 500ML

2kg ripe but good quality blackcurrants
560ml hot water
White caster sugar (the amount depends on the juice yield, see step 5)

---

1. Sterilise all bottles and lids.

2. Wash the fruit well in cold water. Discard any bad or overripe fruit. No need to top and tail as the fruit will be sieved.

3. Place the fruit in a large pan with the hot water. Heat to just boiling and then turn down to a simmer. Allow to simmer for about 5 minutes, then remove from the heat. Mash the fruit well with a potato masher or rolling pin. Replace on the heat, simmer for another 5 minutes and repeat the mashing away from the heat.

4. Use a large fine-meshed sieve or jelly strain bag to strain the juice into a sterile bowl. Leave to strain naturally for as long as you can – at least 4 hours. Then press lightly with the back of a large spoon to ensure as much juice is pressed out as possible. But don't press too hard, as you don't want much of the flesh

to drop into the juice. A little sediment is inevitable and won't make any difference to the finished syrup.

5. The next step is to measure the juice and weigh out the appropriate amount of sugar. For a very sweet, thicker syrup weigh out 75g sugar to every 100ml juice. For a less sweet syrup weigh out 45g to every 100ml juice.

6. The juice will probably be cold by now, so place it in a bowl over a pan of simmering water and stir in the sugar. Continue stirring until the sugar has dissolved.

7. Use a sterile funnel and a jug to pour the syrup into the prepared bottles. Seal them straight away and label with the date and type of syrup. So long as the syrup is stored in the fridge it should keep for 4 weeks unopened, 1 week once opened.

RASPBERRY SYRUP

Make the syrup by following the recipe for Blackcurrant Syrup on page 127, but only simmer the fruit once and instead of adding water, add a squeeze of lemon juice.

STRAWBERRY SYRUP

Make the syrup by following the recipe for Blackcurrant Syrup on page 127, but cut any large strawberries in half and add 100ml water and a squeeze of lemon juice.

ROSEHIP SYRUP

This is a lovely country recipe that is perfect if you have a rosehip bush in your garden or street! We tend not to use rosehips in modern cooking, but they are a great source of vitamin C so it is a shame to let them go to waste. This syrup is a delicious addition to any dessert and goes brilliantly with oranges in Crêpes Suzette.

MAKES ABOUT 3 GIFTS

800g rosehips
1 litre water
400g white caster sugar

1. Sterilise the bottles and lids.

2. Place the rosehips in a blender and chop into small pieces.

3. Place into a pan and pour on the water. Bring to the boil and then simmer for 5 minutes.

4. Remove from the heat and strain the liquid through a fine muslin bag, removing all the pulp but squeezing out the juice.

5. Pour the liquid into a clean pan and bring to the boil. Continue boiling until the liquid reduces by half.

6. Add the sugar and slowly bring back to the boil, allowing the pan to bubble with the lid on for 4–5 minutes. Pour into your sterilised bottles and seal.

CHOCOLATE AND TIA MARIA ICE-CREAM SAUCE

A deliciously moreish and easy sauce that makes a perfect gift which can be tailored to your recipient very easily. It doesn't keep as well as other syrups as it is not boiled, but that won't matter because it won't last long!

MAKES 1 GIFT

100g dark chocolate
50ml Tia Maria (or liqueur of your choice)
150ml double cream
3 tablespoons golden syrup

---

1. Sterilise your bottle and cap.

2. Melt the chocolate in a bowl over a pan of simmering water. Add the liqueur and cream just as the chocolate starts to melt and stir gently with a metal spoon. Remove from the heat.

3. Add the syrup and stir until fully incorporated.

4. Pour into your bottle and devour with good quality ice cream! Try it warm too, you won't regret it!

Alcoholic Fruit and Chocolate Beverages

These are very easy and make spectacular gifts. They do, however, have to be made well in advance and some, such as fruit brandies, need months to mature properly.

You can purchase some really good gift bottles from household stores and online bottles and jars companies. I like to scour the charity and antique shops for old bottles and decanters, so long as they have good fitting lids.

CHERRY BRANDY

MAKES ABOUT 2 X 300ML BOTTLES

800g cherries
200g caster sugar
At least 1 litre brandy

---

1. Sterilise a large screwtop jar, of around 1½ litres, large enough to hold the cherries with room to shake the mixture.

2. Place the cherries in a bowl and pour boiling water over them. Drain straight away and place back in the bowl. Sprinkle the sugar evenly over the fruit and spoon into the jar.

3. Add sufficient brandy to cover the cherries with a couple of centimetres to spare. Screw on the lid and shake the jar for 2–3 minutes to help dissolve the sugar.

4. Store in a dark, cool place and shake the jar every day for 1 week, then leave for 3 months.

5. The jar can be presented like this still containing the cherries, or strain the brandy into another sterile bottle and eat the cherries yourself! It will keep unopened for up to 2 years.

Variations
- Cut the sugar content down to 25g for a much less sweet brandy.
- Double the quantity of sugar to make a very sweet cherry liqueur.

PEACH BRANDY

MAKES ABOUT 2 X 300ML BOTTLES

500g fresh peaches, peeled and halved
750ml brandy
150g sugar

---

1. Sterilise a 1½ litre jar.

2. Place the peaches in a bowl. Pour boiling water over them and then drain immediately.

3. Spoon them into the jar and add the brandy and sugar. Shake the jar well for a few minutes, then leave in a cool, dark place.

4. Leave to mature for about 4 months. It will keep unopened for up to 2 years.

Variations
- Add 300g sugar to the jar to make a peach liqueur.
- Instead of the peaches, place 500g summer fruits along with 150g sugar in the bowl and follow the recipe above. Strain through a fine sieve to remove pips and seeds before spooning into the sterilised jar.
- Plums can be used instead of peaches but if they are Victorias add 250g sugar to the fruit in the bowl and then continue in the same way.

STRAWBERRY GIN LIQUEUR

This liqueur takes about 6 months to mature and be anywhere near ready to drink. So prepare it with really fresh strawberries, which are at the peak of their season and at their cheapest. Use any kind of gin you like in this recipe.

MAKES ABOUT 300ML

500g strawberries
50g caster sugar
250ml gin

1. Sterilise a 1 litre, wide-necked jar with a screwtop. One that is suitable for pickling is ideal.

2. Wash and hull the strawberries and place them in a large roasting pan. Pour over boiling water and then immediately drain.

3. Prick the strawberries once or twice with a fork and sprinkle with a little caster sugar. More caster sugar will mean a sweeter gin liqueur.

4. Place the strawberries in the jar and pack in well. Pour the gin over, covering the strawberries completely, and then screw on the lid.

5. Shake the jar gently and place in a cool, dark place for 1 week. Shake again and leave for 6 months.

6. Sterilise the bottles you wish to present the liqueur in. 500g strawberries will yield approx 295ml liqueur.

7. Strain the liquor from the strawberries. I find using a jam-making bag is the most efficient way of straining the fruit from

the liquor, but a cheesecloth or muslin will also do. A sieve allows too many bits through – it needs to be as clear as possible.

8. Fill the sterilised bottles with the liqueur and seal with the lids. It will keep unopened for up to 2 years.

Variation
• Replace the strawberries with raspberries, but there is no need to prick them before bottling.

MARMALADE GIN

Amazingly easy to make and very delicious, this reminds me of Cointreau and is stunning used in Crêpes Suzette. It is a fantastic boozy addition to any orange pudding or sauce, and works really well with duck dishes to give a kick!

MAKES ABOUT 1 LITRE

300g good quality marmalade
100g caster sugar
200ml fresh orange juice
Approx 400ml gin

1. Sterilise a 1 litre, wide-necked jar or Kilner jar.

2. Put the marmalade in a pan with the sugar and heat gently until the marmalade is runny. Don't boil and don't worry about dissolving the sugar.

3. Pour the mixture into the prepared jar and add the orange juice. Shake gently to mix. Pour in the gin to top up the jar and screw on or secure the lid.

4. Shake gently to mix all the ingredients and store in a cool, dark place for 4 weeks.

5. Taste and add more sugar if necessary. Leave for 1 more week.

6. Strain using a jam-making bag, or otherwise a cheesecloth or muslin, and then pour the clear gin liqueur into sterile bottles of your choice. It will keep unopened for up to 2 years.

Luxury Chocolate Liqueur

This is very easy to make and gives a silky smooth finish to the creamy chocolate liqueur. I prefer to use brandy in this recipe, but you can use vodka if you prefer. The condensed milk sweetens and thickens the drink so it means you do not need to add any more sugar.

MAKES ABOUT 1½ LITRES

500ml whole milk
150g dark chocolate, broken up into small pieces
200ml condensed milk
300ml single cream
500ml brandy or vodka

1. Sterilise either 2 x 750ml bottles or 3 x 500ml bottles and their caps.

2. Put the milk in a pan and heat until it boils. Then turn the heat right down to very low.

3. Add the chocolate and stir gently until it has all melted. Remove from the heat and allow to cool for 10 minutes.

4. Stir in the condensed milk and the cream. Don't be tempted to whisk – you don't want bubbles in the liquid.

5. Add the brandy or vodka in three or four stages, stirring continuously.

6. When completely cold, carefully decant into the bottles using a sterile funnel. Secure the lids immediately and label and date the bottles.

7. Store in a cool, dark place. It will keep for 2–3 months unopened.

Useful Tip
Why not make up a batch of the Marmalade Gin and give them with this luxury liqueur for a chocolate orange treat!

CHOCOLATE LIQUEUR

This is a lighter version of the Luxury Chocolate Liqueur – not as creamy, but still very sweet and chocolatey. It does require some ageing as it uses cocoa powder instead of chocolate.

MAKES ABOUT 1 LITRE

300g caster sugar
150ml milk
50ml water
80g cocoa powder
700ml vodka
1 teaspoon vanilla extract

1. Sterilise a 1 litre (or larger), lidded glass jar.

2. Put the sugar, milk and water in a pan and heat gently, stirring continuously, until all the sugar has dissolved. Stir the cocoa in vigorously, then bring to the boil. As soon as it is boiling reduce the heat and simmer for 3 minutes.

3. Allow to cool, then stir in the vodka and vanilla extract. Pour into the glass jar and secure the lid. Shake well.

4. Leave in a cool, dark place for 8 days. Shake every day until the eighth day when the grains of cocoa powder will have fallen to the bottom of the solution.

5. Using a jam-making bag, or otherwise a cheesecloth or muslin, strain the liqueur into a sterile jug leaving behind the small grains.

6. Fill 2 x 500ml sterilised bottles with the liqueur and leave to mature for 2–3 weeks.

COFFEE LIQUEUR

This is again very easy to make and gives a strong coffee taste. I like to heat the coffee beans for 5 minutes in a hot oven before adding to the vodka as it enhances the strength of flavour.

MAKES ABOUT 1.5 LITRES

100g coffee beans
1 litre vodka
300g soft brown sugar
200ml boiling water

---

1. Place the coffee beans and vodka in a lidded jug or pan and stir. Then cover and leave for 48 hours.

2. Test to see if the vodka has taken on sufficient coffee flavour. If it isn't strong enough, leave for another 24 hours.

3. When you are happy with the strength of flavour, put the sugar and boiling water in a pan and stir over a low heat. When the sugar has dissolved, simmer for 2 minutes then allow to cool.

4. Stir the syrup into the vodka and leave to infuse for 24 hours.

5. Sterilise 3 x 500ml bottles.

6. Strain the liqueur into the bottles using a jam-making bag, or otherwise a cheesecloth or muslin. It should keep for 6 months.

LIMONCELLO

This is the taste of Italian sunshine and is very easy to make. Always use unwaxed lemons, large Sicilian ones are ideal as they have very thick peel which is easy to zest. The flavour of the oil and juice gives an authentic rich lemon flavour to the drink.

MAKES ABOUT 1.5 LITRES

6 large unwaxed lemons
500g caster sugar
400ml boiling water
1 litre vodka

1. Carefully pare away the zest from the lemon skin. Leave all the white pith behind as this makes the drink very bitter, even a small amount.

2. Put the zest, sugar and boiling water in a pan and stir well over a low heat. When the sugar has dissolved, simmer for 15 minutes. Then cover and leave to cool.

3. Juice the lemons and when the syrup is cool add the lemon juice and vodka.

4. Either cover the pan or transfer the whole lot into a large lidded jar or jug and leave to infuse for a week, stored in a cold, dark place. Shake every day.

5. Sterilise 3 x 500ml bottles or 2 x 750ml bottles.

6. Strain the limoncello through a fine sieve and transfer to the bottles.

7. Allow to mature for 1 more week then either drink or give it as a gift. It should keep for at least 6 months.

Variation
• You can make any citrus liqueur by replacing the lemons with oranges, limes or grapefruit. If you are feeling particularly fruity, try a combination.

Chapter Nine
Presenting Your Sweets and Treats

The simplest gift can be made extra special with a little planning and careful preparation. Of course, a touch of inspiration helps too, so make sure you visit those delicious looking chocolateries for ideas and hints for creating your own sweets and treats to give away.

This chapter gives you some tips on presentation and packaging. Turn to page 146 for stockists information, though you will generally find everything you need in your local craft shop.

Jars

The humble glass jar has a lot to be proud of. Not only does it keep your hard work fresh and intact, but it also looks lovely. Jars can be spruced up very easily, and recycled jars need only a lick of paint to make them look fabulous. You can buy jars in bulk from online retailers if you are looking to make a lot – have a look at the list of Stockists, for more information.

Recycling Old Jars

Make sure you use a jar that doesn't have any logos embossed into the glass, so as not to give the game away. Cheaper jars from supermarket-own brand jam are particularly good. Remove all labels by soaking in warm soapy water for an hour and scrubbing off the excess glue.

Sterilise the jars using sterilising fluid or by boiling them in a large pan of water for 10 minutes. Don't forget you will need to sterilise the lids too.

A can of enamel spray paint can make short work of decorating the lids. To keep costs down, choose one colour you like and spray a batch of lids ready for use at a later date. Alternatively, you can paint the jars with enamel-based paints. Leave them to dry completely before sterilising again to ensure they are safe to use.

Cloth tops

A lovely, traditional way of presenting your jar is with a circle of fabric placed over the top, secured with an elastic band and a small piece of thin ribbon. You can use most thin fabrics (even cutting up an old shirt for the job, though make sure you wash it first!), but a nice, printed cotton works best. Simply measure the diameter of your lid and make a template out of thick card that is double the diameter. Pinking shears will give a decorative edge and are available from all craft shops fairly inexpensively.

Ribbon ties work best with 5–10mm ribbon. For a nice, neat bow, you will need a length of ribbon roughly 2½ times the circumference of the jar. Simply wrap the ribbon round the jar 2½ times and cut to size.

Decorative Jars

A lovely way to present your sweeties is in an old-fashioned sweet jar. These are available from eBay, second-hand shops and some online retailers. Alternatively, pop to your local sweet shop and ask if they have any spare you could buy. They are usually much cheaper than vintage ones.

Kilner jars are particularly decorative and are available from most supermarkets. They need very little else other than a large piece of ribbon tied round the top. Try and use a contrasting colour to the contents, so for barley sugars use a bright green or pink, chocolates a purple, and so on.

Bottles

Bottles for liqueurs can be absolutely gorgeous. If you're feeling generous, take a trip to your local antique shop and treat your recipient to a lovely vintage glass bottle. Decorative glass bottles need very little else doing to them, though you will have to scrupulously sterilise them as who knows how many spiders have been sleeping inside since their last use!

Old bottles look fantastic as a decorative feature in a bathroom or kitchen. It can be quite addictive to scour charity and antique shops for decorative examples, though too many and your cupboard may end up looking like a potions store cupboard.

Boxes

There are many sizes of gift box available for your homemade treats, though a particularly useful one is the book box, which is designed to fit a paperback book inside and houses chocolates very nicely. Simply arrange them in petit four cases and use a little shredded crepe paper to pad them out – this is particularly important if you are going to post the box.

You can also make your own box fairly easily using some stiff cardboard. You can either make a smaller lid or simply wrap the box in cellophane for a gorgeous gift for any occasion.

Handmade Sweetie Packets

A great way to make a really professional-looking gift is to use cellophane bags. Simply place your sweeties in the bag and make a card topper to secure them. Create your topper by measuring the width of your bag and adding 5mm. Cut out a square using this measurement and fold it in half. Place the topper over the open edge of the bag and staple it closed. Try and space the staples so they are even on both sides. It is a lovely idea to get the children to decorate the toppers.

Mugs

An inexpensive white mug (or large cup and saucer) filled with homemade sweets can make a wonderful instant present, finished with a bit of cellophane wrapping. You can buy this in rolls from craft shops (though we have found large rolls very inexpensively online, see the list of Stockists for more detail) and it lends any gift instant appeal. Simply cut a large piece (much larger than would just cover your present) and place your mug in the centre. Gather the cellophane around the mug and twist it closed. Secure this with lots of ribbon (the curling ribbon widely available works brilliantly) and trim off the excess. A homemade tag will finish off your gift perfectly.

Hampers

There is nothing quite like the joy of receiving a homemade hamper, and hopefully this book will enable you to make a sweet one of your own. A few muffins, a box of fudge, a jar of sweets, a jar of jam and a bottle of liqueur housed in a wicker basket is a brilliant option for those very-difficult-to-buy-for friends and family members. A little shredded wrapping paper or newspaper in the bottom makes a brilliant nest – simply lay out your goodies and cellophane wrap like there's no tomorrow. This also makes the present look larger than it is, so is perfect if you're a bit light on content!

Labels

The varieties of labels available are endless, but they are very simple to make. If you're not too hot with a computer, a simple piece of brown paper and a bit of calligraphy works just as well!

Investing in a pack of good quality paper for printing on will help dramatically. Cheap copy paper from the supermarket will not only make your hard work look inferior, but can easily get smudged when wet. You can buy specialist jam labels from most craft shops. Check the list of Stockists for more information.

Stockists

The Range
Branches nationwide
www.therange.co.uk
tel: 0845 026 7598

Hobby Craft
Branches nationwide
www.hobbycraft.co.uk
tel: 0845 051 6599

Lakeland
Branches nationwide
www.lakeland.co.uk
tel: 015394 88100

Sugarshack
Unit 12
Bowmans Trading Estate
Westoreland Road
London NW9 9RL
www.sugarshack.co.uk
tel: 020 8204 2994

Cake Craft Shop
Unit 8
North Downs Business Park
Pilgrims Way (Lime Pit Lane)
Sevenoaks
Kent TN13 2TL
www.cakecraftshop.co.uk
tel: 01732 463 573

Jane Asher Party Cakes &
    Sugarcraft
22–24 Cale Street
London SW3 3QU
www.janeasher.com
tel: 020 7584 6177

FMM Sugarcraft
Unit 7, Chancerygate
Business Park
Whiteleaf Road
Hemel Hempstead
Herts HP3 9HD
www.fmmsugarcraft.com
tel: 01442 292970

Sugarcraft Supplies
1 Sycamore Court
Lotherton Way
Garforth
Leeds LS25 2JY
www.sugarcraft-supplies.co.uk
tel: 0871 789 5595

Jam Jar Shop
B1 Broadlands
Heywood
Lancashire OL10 2TS
www.jamjarshop.com

Preserve Shop Ltd
Bridge House
Backbarrow
Ulverston
Cumbria LA12 8PZ
www.preserveshop.co.uk

Patteson's Glass Ltd
No. 25 Atlas House
Estate Road 8
South Humberside
Industrial Estate
Grimsby
N.E. Lincolnshire DN31 2TG
www.jarsandbottles-store.co.uk
tel: 01472 340005

Index